THE POSTMODERN

How can one understand the nature of the present?
What might it mean to say the world has become postmodern?

In this book, Simon Malpas introduces a range of key theorists and theories that have, under the banner of the postmodern, sought in different ways to explore art, culture and the nature of thought in the contemporary world. He examines some of the most important and influential definitions of the postmodern, and uses straightforward examples and illustrations to explore their implications for such areas as identity, history, art, literature, culture and politics.

The Postmodern builds up a picture of the key contemporary debates about postmodernism and postmodernity, enabling readers to begin to approach the primary texts of postmodern theory and culture with confidence.

Simon Malpas is Lecturer in English Literature at Edinburgh University. He is author of *Jean-François Lyotard* (Routledge) and has edited *Postmodern Debates* (Palgrave) and *The New Aestheticism* (MUP).

THE NEW CRITICAL IDIOM

SERIES EDITOR: JOHN DRAKAKIS, UNIVERSITY OF STIRLING

The New Critical Idiom is an invaluable series of introductory guides to today's critical terminology. Each book

- provides a handy, explanatory guide to the use (and abuse) of the term
- offers an original and distinctive overview by a leading literary and cultural critic
- relates the term to the larger field of cultural representation.

With a strong emphasis on clarity, lively debate and the widest possible breadth of examples, *The New Critical Idiom* is an indispensable approach to key topics in literary studies.

Also available in this series:

THE POSTMODERN

Simon Malpas

Routledge
Taylor & Francis Group

LONDON AND NEW YORK

First published 2005
by Routledge
2 Park Square, Milton Park, Abingdon, Oxon OX14 4RN

Simultaneously published in the USA and Canada
by Routledge
270 Madison Ave, New York, NY 10016

Routledge is an imprint of the Taylor & Francis Group

© 2005 Simon Malpas

Typeset in Garamond and Scala Sans by
Keystroke, Jacaranda Lodge, Wolverhampton
Printed and bound in Great Britain by
TJ International Ltd, Padstow, Cornwall

British Library Cataloguing in Publication Data
A catalogue record for this book is available from the British Library

Library of Congress Cataloging in Publication Data
Malpas, Simon.
    The postmodern / Simon Malpas.
        p. cm. — (New critical idiom)
    Includes bibliographical references and index.
    ISBN 0–415–28064–8 (alk. paper) — ISBN 0–415–28065–6 (pbk. : alk.
    paper)
    1. Postmodernism. I. Title. II. Series.
    B831.2.M35 2005
    149'.97—dc22   2004007792

ISBN 0–415–28064–8 (hbk)
ISBN 0–415–28065–6 (pbk)

CONTENTS

SERIES EDITOR'S PREFACE

The New Critical Idiom is a series of introductory books which seeks to extend the lexicon of literary terms, in order to address the radical changes which have taken place in the study of literature during the last decades of the twentieth century. The aim is to provide clear, well-illustrated accounts of the full range of terminology currently in use, and to evolve histories of its changing usage.

The current state of the discipline of literary studies is one where there is considerable debate concerning basic questions of terminology. This involves, among other things, the boundaries which distinguish the literary from the non-literary; the position of literature within the larger sphere of culture; the relationship between literatures of different cultures; and questions concerning the relation of literary to other cultural forms within the context of interdisciplinary studies.

It is clear that the field of literary criticism and theory is a dynamic and heterogeneous one. The present need is for individual volumes on terms which combine clarity of exposition with an adventurousness of perspective and a breadth of application. Each volume will contain as part of its apparatus some indication of the direction in which the definition of particular terms is likely to move, as well as expanding the disciplinary boundaries within which some of these terms have been traditionally contained. This will involve some re-situation of terms within the larger field of cultural representation, and will introduce examples from the area of film and the modern media in addition to examples from a variety of literary texts.

ACKNOWLEDGEMENTS

I should like to thank John Drakakis and Liz Thompson for their encouragement, support and acute editorial commentary. Without their assistance, this project would not have been completed. The book owes many of its arguments and ideas to colleagues and students in the English Department at Manchester Metropolitan University. In particular, I should like to thank Barry Atkins, who not only encouraged me to write it in the first place but also commented on the early drafts of the manuscript; Erikka Askeland, who offered advice about contemporary art and helped to track down some of the key media sources; Kate McGowan, Jules Townsend and Paul Wake, who each read and commented helpfully on sections of the text; and Michael Bradshaw, Huw Jones, Rob Lapsley, Julie Waddington and Sue Zlosnik, who offered support and gave their time to discuss many of the book's arguments. Without their advice and always-constructive criticism, this would not be the book that it now is.

The table on pages 7–8 is from Ihab Hassan, *The Dismemberment of Orpheus* © 1982. Reprinted by permission of The University of Wisconsin Press.

INTRODUCTION
The Plurality of the Postmodern

What is it like to be postmodern?

Contemporary culture moves at an almost incomprehensible speed. The opportunities and lifestyles open to people in Europe and North America seem to multiply exponentially as new ideas, technologies and fashions appear at ever-increasing rates. Space and time shrink almost to nothing as we move around the world at breakneck pace. Civilisations, traditions and forms of social interaction are transformed or even annihilated as borders become more fluid and the conventions, customs and ways of life that once distinguished one place from another turn into matters of choice for an internationalised consumer. The world is now, quite literally, at our fingertips as we choose and purchase lifestyles from wherever we please, eclectically piecing together patchworks of images and signs to produce our identities. This shrinking of the world is not just a result of the physical movements of jet-setting businesspeople and package holidaymakers, but even more a consequence of the culture created by the mobile phone users who are always 'in touch', the television viewers who are fed stories from around the globe almost at the instant that they occur, and the internet surfers who can access the most up-to-the-minute, arcane or even bizarre information from any corner of the planet at the push of a button. We inhabit a multinational, multi-media, interdependent world marketplace, and have been, to use a contemporary buzzword that will be explored in more detail later in the book, 'globalised'. In the words of the French postmodern theorist Jean-François Lyotard, we now live in a world where

> Eclecticism is the degree zero of contemporary general culture: you listen to reggae; you watch a western; you eat McDonald's at midday and local cuisine at night; you wear Paris perfume in Tokyo and dress retro in Hong Kong; knowledge is the stuff of TV game shows. . . . Together, artist, gallery owner, critic, and public indulge one another in the Anything Goes – it is time to relax.
>
> (1992: 8)

There are some critics who might see this account of an 'anything goes' culture that freely chooses from and mixes ideas and fashions from around the world as the essence of postmodernism. We can all relax into our multi-cultural postmodern world where even the most obscure desire can, with a bit of imagination, quickly be satisfied.

But there is another postmodern world, one that coexists uneasily with this one and acts almost as its inverted image. Lyotard's argument continues:

> this realism of Anything Goes is the realism of money. . . . This realism accommodates every tendency just as capitalism accommodates every 'need' – so long as these tendencies and needs have buying power.
>
> (1992: 8)

Contemporary culture in all its variety rests on 'money', on 'buying power', and the apparently borderless postmodern world is so only for the Western elites who have the wealth and power to travel, consume and freely choose their lifestyles. In stark contrast to them stand the dispossessed peoples of those parts of the planet for which globalisation seems often to mean a loss of security and self-determination rather than an expansion of opportunity. In the West, many customary forms of employment have vanished as companies move abroad to areas where labour is less expensive or less regulated, often leaving behind them communities bereft of occupation, wealth and self-worth. In the developing world local resources have been bought up by international corporations and whole peoples have become subject to the violent fluctuations of world markets without the safeguard of Western systems of welfare support that might protect them from destitution or even starvation during an economic downturn. For these groups the consumer lifestyles of the rich are little more than fantasies or hopeless aspirations. In contrast to the international travellers, the world is also filled with refugees and asylum seekers striving to cross the more and more tightly patrolled borders of the richer nations as they struggle from the poverty, danger and oppression of their homelands to those countries that seem to hold out the promise of freedom and prosperity.

Together with the postmodernism of lifestyle and consumer choice there is, necessarily, another postmodernism: that of deregulation, dispersal and disruption as the securities of tradition and community are continually crushed. Between these two contemporary extremes, a conflict exists which threatens the stability of both. The role of the postmodern thinker or artist must be to explore and question this contemporary situation, to grasp the opportunities it might offer and respond to its challenges.

The aim of this book is to introduce a range of the key theorists and theories that have, under the banner of the postmodern, sought in different ways to do this. It will look at some of the most important and influential definitions of the postmodern, and explore their implications for such areas as identity, history, art, literature, culture and politics. Through doing this, it will build up a picture of postmodernism and postmodernity that will allow readers to begin to approach the primary texts of postmodern theory and culture with confidence. It will also try to make a case that this postmodern theory and culture provide important means by which one can understand the opportunities and challenges that today's globalised world presents us with.

DEFINING THE POSTMODERN

It would be nice to be able to begin with a straightforward definition of the postmodern, one that sums it up and grasps, in its essence, what it is all about. This definition could then be explained and developed to provide a broad basis for an understanding of the phenomenon that would show how it is relevant to contemporary culture and important for the future. The explanation might helpfully locate the postmodern within a more general idea of culture and provide clues about the ways in which one can comment upon, say, the narrative structures of postmodern novels, the political implications of postmodern art or architecture, and the importance of an understanding of postmodernism and postmodernity for contemporary social and political theory in a rapidly changing world.

Unfortunately, finding such a simple, uncontroversial meaning for the term 'postmodern' is all but impossible. In fact, as we shall see, this sort of clear and concise process of identification and definition is one of the key elements of rationality that the postmodern sets out to challenge. In our day-to-day lives, we expect common sense and accessibility. From the perspectives of scientific reason or philosophical logic, clarity and precision should be the sole aim of thought. But postmodernism, in contrast, often seeks to grasp what escapes these processes of definition and celebrates what resists or disrupts them. It would therefore follow that not only might such a simple definition miss the complexities of the postmodern, it would also be in danger of undermining the basic tenets of what makes it such a radical and exciting area of contemporary critical thought and artistic practice.

In the light of this, defining the postmodern can seem an intractable problem. But things are even more difficult than this. Few critics even agree about what exactly it is that they are dealing with. There is little consensus among its numerous supporters and detractors about what the postmodern might be, which aspects of culture, thought and society it relates to, and how it might or might not provide ways to comprehend the contemporary world. Rather than too little evidence, there is too much that has been brought to bear in the discussions, debates and frequently furious arguments that have attempted to determine what exactly postmodernism and postmodernity are about. The opposition with which this book began is just one example of this: some critics celebrate the postmodern as a period of playful freedom and consumer choice, some see it as a culture that has gone off the rails as communities around the globe have their traditions obliterated by the spread of capitalism, and for others its complex theories and outlandish cultural productions mark an abdication from any engagement with the real world at all. This plurality of definitions has become crucial to the sense that the term 'postmodern' now carries, and it is important if one is to begin to understand it, therefore, to grasp both its multifaceted nature and its propensity to open up debate between the various parties that have a stake in its definition.

If this book is to introduce postmodernism and postmodernity it will, therefore, also have to explore some of those different versions of the postmodern, work through their implications and present an account of the key roles they play in a range of contemporary debates. As part of this process it will discuss some of the most important thinkers, artists and texts of the last fifty years and provide those who are less familiar with recent critical theory with a map of the postmodern territory that should allow them to make their own decisions about its meaning, validity and importance.

POSTMODERNISMS AND POSTMODERNITIES

For many people, the mere mention of the word 'postmodernism' brings immediately to mind ideas of fracturing, fragmentation, indeterminacy and plurality, all of which are indeed key postmodern figures. However, before looking in detail at the various critical discussions about what postmodernism might have to say about these ideas, it is important to recognise that postmodernity is itself already a discourse that is fractured and fragmentary. Although many of the literary, cultural and artistic movements that have come to be called postmodern can be traced back to the 1950s and 1960s, and even by some critics to much earlier than this (see Bertens (1995) for a detailed account of the historical genesis of the term 'postmodern'), it was in the late 1970s, the 1980s and the early 1990s that the terms 'postmodernism' and 'postmodernity' became pervasive in European and North American culture. There was a brief period during these three decades when every new work, event and innovation was liable to be described as postmodern, when the news media employed the term on an almost daily basis and the presses of academic publishers seemed constantly to be churning out new and different books and articles describing it and applying it to phenomena from across the cultural spectrum. From Cabbage Patch Kid dolls to chaos theory, Band Aid to war in the Balkans, almost everything that emerged on the cultural scene at the time was hailed as being in one way or another a new instance of the postmodern. In recent years, the postmodern has seemed less omnipresent, and yet the concepts, ideas and categories deployed by its exponents are still crucial to many of the key debates in contemporary culture. Although not reducible to them, postmodern thought has interacted, and continues to interact, with feminism and queer theory, postcolonialism and the politics of globalisation, as well as with such areas as environmental studies, history, philosophy and literary criticism.

Because it was taken up as a buzzword to define the spirit of the times by the media as well as in so many different disciplines within the university, the multiple analyses and accounts of it are irreducible to the language of a particular subject area or mode of thought. In fact, one of its most radical characteristics has been the way in which during the past few decades it has often broken down the barriers between areas of academic study, bringing them into new forms of collaboration or conflict. The postmodern has become a key category in disciplines from across the Humanities. Its meaning for students of literature, however, is often very different from the ways it is deployed by theologians, philosophers, political scientists, historians or sociologists, as each discipline draws its own senses of postmodernism and postmodernity into debates within their respective subject areas. Even after the media frenzy about postmodernism died out in the mid-1990s, discussions within these disciplines have continued apace, and have led to a range of differently constructed postmodernisms and postmodernities. In this complex mixture of ideas and movements, it is all but impossible to generate agreement between critics about precisely what postmodernism or postmodernity might be. What is certain, however, is that, in whatever ways the terms are employed by critics, it has vital things to tell us about how we engage with and are shaped by our cultural milieu today.

As a means of thinking about the contemporary world, the postmodern has been defined in a huge variety of different ways: as a new aesthetic formation (Hassan, 1982, 1987), a condition (Lyotard, 1984; Harvey, 1990), a culture (Connor, 1997), a cultural dominant (Jameson, 1991), a set of artistic movements employing a parodic mode of self-conscious representation (Hutcheon, 1988, 2002), an ethical or political imperative (Bauman, 1993, 1995), a period in which we have reached the 'end of history' (Baudrillard, 1994; Fukuyama, 1992; Vattimo, 1988), a 'new horizon of our cultural, philosophical and political experience' (Laclau, 1988), an 'illusion' (Eagleton, 1996), a reactionary political formation (Callinicos, 1989), or even just a rather unfortunate mistake (Norris, 1990, 1993). It evokes ideas of irony, disruption, difference, discontinuity, playfulness, parody, hyper-reality and simulation. It has been, for some, a radicalisation of modern art that has pushed avant-garde experimentation to new limits, and for others a democratisation of cultural studies that has allowed critics to pay as much attention to, and place as much value in, popular entertainment as it does the old masters. For others still, postmodern art and culture are simply surface phenomena generated by much more far-reaching social, political or philosophical transformations that have taken place in the modern world.

One of the first writers to employ the term 'postmodern' was the American literary critic Ihab Hassan. In the second edition of his groundbreaking book from 1971, *The Dismemberment of Orpheus: Toward a Postmodern Literature* (1982), he produces a schematic list of differences between modernism and postmodernism. This list purports to present the changes in focus between modern and postmodern art in terms of the wider questions they raise about representation. Although many of the categories it introduces have remained highly controversial, it is worth reproducing here as a guide:

Modernism	*Postmodernism*
Romanticism/Symbolism	Pataphysics/Dadaism
Form (conjunctive, closed)	Antiform (disjunctive, open)
Purpose	Play
Design	Chance
Hierarchy	Anarchy
Mastery/Logos	Exhaustion/Silence
Art object/Finished work	Process/Performance/Happening
Distance	Participation
Creation/Totalization	Decreation/Deconstruction
Synthesis	Antithesis
Presence	Absence
Centring	Dispersal

Genre/Boundary	Text/Intertext
Semantics	Rhetoric
Paradigm	Syntagm
Hypotaxis	Parataxis
Metaphor	Metonymy
Selection	Combination
Root/Depth	Rhizome/Surface
Interpretation/Reading	Against Interpretation/Misreading
Signified	Signifier
Lisible (readerly)	*Scriptible* (writerly)
Narrative/*Grande histoire*	Antinarrative/*Petite histoire*
Master code	Idiolect
Symptom	Desire
Type	Mutant
Genital/Phallic	Polymorphous/Androgynous
Paranoia	Schizophrenia
Origin/Cause	Difference – differance/trace
God the Father	The Holy Ghost
Metaphysics	Irony
Determinacy	Indeterminacy
Transcendence	Immanence

(Hassan, 1982: 267–8)

Many of these terms will be unfamiliar to readers, not all have remained central to definitions of the postmodern by other critics, and some have been strongly resisted. And even this list, lengthy and complicated as it might appear, is far from exhaustive: the descriptions and definitions could go on and on. Hassan, moreover, pointedly problematises his own categories by arguing that, 'the dichotomies this table represents remain insecure, equivocal. For differences shift, defer, even collapse . . . and inversions and exceptions, in both modernism and postmodernism, abound' (Hassan, 1982: 269). Broadly speaking, however, the key difference between the two columns can be located in the closure and rigid organisation of those terms listed under modernism (with ideas such as 'form', 'hierarchy', 'mastery' and 'determinacy') against the openness of those linked to postmodernism (with its 'play', 'chance', 'dispersal', 'combination', 'difference' and 'desire'). As we shall see in later chapters, this straightforward opposition is extremely problematic and overly reductive of the different interactions between the modern and the post-modern, but it gives a very clear sense of the excitement and attempted radicalism of the latter movement. What the list also demonstrates quite helpfully is that stylistic, literary and philosophical categories are intermixed in any definition of postmodernism or postmodernity. Although Hassan's own discussion focuses throughout on literary culture, the mixture of different categories he includes in this list displays the interdependence of art, philosophy, politics, psychology and social analysis in postmodern thought.

The postmodern appears, then, to have had a stake in almost every area of intellectual enquiry during the last third of a century, and yet each of the manifestations mentioned here, all of which will be discussed in much more detail in the forthcoming chapters, has had a different focus and impact. As the last paragraphs suggest, the term 'postmodern' tends to be employed in critical writing in two key ways: either as 'postmodernism' or 'postmodernity'. This distinction has often proved to be the most basic fracture within the whole fragmentary postmodern discourse. Broadly speaking, postmodernism has tended to focus on questions of style and artistic representation, and postmodernity has been employed to designate a specific cultural context or historical epoch. So, for example, Salman Rushdie's novel *Midnight's Children* (1981) with its playful style, its mixture of popular and arcane reference and fragmentary narrative structure, might be taken as an instance of postmodernism in literature, while Jean-François Lyotard's arguments about the transformation of the nature and status of knowledge and the politics of technological innovation in *The Postmodern Condition* (1984) and *The Inhuman* (1991) have been received as contributions to a theory of postmodernity. Postmodernism is thus often described as a style or a genre, while postmodernity is said to refer to an epoch or period.

A firm and fast distinction between postmodernism as a style and postmodernity as a period is, of course, impossible. However, for the purpose of beginning to introduce what is at stake in the postmodern, the first two chapters of this book will retain their separation. Chapter 1 will explore cultural postmodernism through discussions of architecture, art and literature, while Chapter 2 will set postmodernism in its broader social and political contexts by introducing some of the key theories of postmodernity. The second part of the book begins to break down this distinction to show how the two terms are inextricably but problematically interrelated. In Chapters 3, 4 and 5, the often tense relations between modernity and postmodernity, modernism and postmodernism will be investigated by focusing on three specific areas: the questions of subjectivity and identity, the ways in which history and progress are understood, and the possibilities of political resistance that modern and postmodern thought might offer. Taken as a whole, the aim of this book is to demonstrate the importance of the postmodern, and to introduce the challenging ways in which it seeks to transform our ideas of culture, society, politics and philosophy.

1

MODERNISM AND POSTMODERNISM

The American architectural theorist and critic Charles Jencks makes the following claim in the introduction to his book, *What is Post-Modernism?*:

> Post-Modernism is now a world-wide movement in all the arts and disciplines. Post-modern politics varies from the conviction politics of Margaret Thatcher and Tony Blair to the search for a new liberalism that can combine multiculturalism and universal rights; post-modern food varies from Cambozola (Camembert and Gorgonzola improved by combining) to California Cuisine (French plus Pacific Rim plus supposedly healthy). There are more books on Post-Modernism than its parent Modernism, which is not to say that it is more mature or better, but just here to stay. We are well past the age where we can merely accept or reject this new 'ism'; it is too omnipresent for either approach.
>
> (Jencks, 1996: 6)

For Jencks, postmodernism is the style of our age, and a particularly contradictory one at that. From global politics to fashionable cuisine, postmodernism is 'omnipresent' in all aspects of contemporary culture, and particularly in the arts. Because of this ubiquity it is difficult to categorise according to a simple set of rules or attributes. The aim of this chapter is to introduce some of the key ways in which it has manifested itself in contemporary theories and cultural practices by examining a number of important arguments that have recently been produced about architecture, art and literature.

Postmodernism, with its focus on style and modes of representation, is often read as a successor to modernism, the collection of literary and cultural movements that emerged across Europe and North America during the second half of the nineteenth century and the first half of the twentieth. There are modernisms in literature, music, art, theatre, dance, architecture and even photography. Again, as with the multiplicity of postmodernisms, the problem that faces the critic is that each of these is different from each of the others, and some (such as literature, art and music) even have multiple strands within their own modernisms which each lead in turn to more forms of postmodernism.

Because of the plurality of modernisms and postmodernisms that cover all aspects of artistic and cultural practice, this section will not attempt to provide an all-encompassing definition of the whole movement but will rather take two examples from different postmodern cultural theories, architecture and art, and show how they come to interact with the theories of modernism they seek to supersede. Neither discussion intends to be exhaustive of the possibilities or seeks to include all of the trends of modernism and postmodernism in either field. The aim is rather to identify the ways in which different versions of the postmodern emerge from modernism and to begin to illustrate how postmodernist theory might relate to contemporary cultural practice. It is important to remember, though, that postmodernism as a style is also developed in the works themselves, and, to illustrate this, the third discussion of postmodernism will focus on a particular literary text, Alasdair Gray's novel *Poor Things*, to show how three critics of postmodern literature might approach it.

The fourth section takes a different tack: it explores an argument put forward by a number of critics that, if postmodernism is a formal or stylistic category, its impact can be identified in works from earlier periods too, and it might therefore be seen as something other than just a contemporary phenomenon. The aim of the chapter is thus to introduce a representative sample of the varieties of postmodernist theory and practice in order to give an overview of the field that can be developed in more detail as the book progresses.

ARCHITECTURE: MODERNISM AND POSTMODERNISM

Many introductions to postmodernism begin with a discussion of its role in architecture. There are a number of reasons for this. First, architectural style has an immediate impact upon people's day-to-day lives: the environments in which they live, travel and work can deeply affect how people view themselves, relate to each other and experience the world. Second, because of the need for architects to attract large sums of money in the form of grants or commissions to complete their projects, the tenets of architectural postmodernism are helpfully theorised by a range of eloquent writers who employ accessible, non-specialist language to provide clear definitions of its forms, aims and ideals. Third, and most importantly for introductions to a more general idea of postmodernism, in architecture the postmodern movement has a very precise notion of the modernism that it is 'post'.

Architectural modernism manifested itself in the form of the International Style that grew up in the aftermath of the First World War and became pervasive in the post-Second World War reconstruction of Europe. The International Style was a movement that sought to renew the processes of building and design by eschewing traditional *ad hoc* environments in favour of a universal architectural grammar in which business and housing developments would follow the same rules whether they were produced in Manchester or Massachusetts, Berlin or Bangkok. This new architecture would be rationally organised and functional, use up-to-date materials such as glass, concrete and steel and refuse to resort to what many modern architects perceived to be unnecessary ornamentation. According to an important architectural manifesto from 1928, which was signed by many of the leading European modernists, 'It is urgently necessary for architecture . . . to rely upon the present realities of industrial technology, even though such an attitude must perforce lead to products fundamentally different from those of past epochs' (Conrads, 1970: 110). The new industrial cities needed new forms of accommodation and organisation, and the International Style of modernist architecture set out to provide them: the town was to become 'a working tool' (Conrads, 1970: 89) that allowed for the smooth running and efficient administration of working life.

Charles Jencks, who is perhaps the most influential theorist of architectural postmodernism, provides a straightforward and lively account of the move from this International Style modernism to postmodernism at the beginning of his book, *The Language of Post-Modern Architecture*:

> Happily, we can date the death of Modern Architecture to a precise moment in time. Unlike the death of a person, which is becoming a complex affair of brain waves versus heartbeats, Modern Architecture went out with a bang. . . . Modern Architecture died in St Louis, Missouri on July 15, 1972 at 3.32 pm (or thereabouts) when the infamous Pruitt-Igoe scheme, or rather several of its slab blocks, were given the final *coup de grace* by dynamite. Previously it had been vandalised, mutilated and defaced by its black inhabitants, and although millions of dollars were pumped back, trying to keep it alive (fixing the broken elevators, repairing smashed windows, repainting), it was finally put out of its misery. Boom, boom, boom.
>
> (Jencks, 1991: 23)

Pruitt-Igoe was a modern housing development like many of the tower blocks and high-rise estates that can still be seen in the cities of Europe and North America, often in the poorer districts and frequently in rundown and vandalised states. It consisted, according to Jencks, of 'slab blocks fourteen storeys high with rational "streets in the air" (which were safe from cars, but as it turned out not safe from crime)'. It employed 'a separation of pedestrian and vehicular traffic, the provision of play space, and local amenities such as laundries, crèches and gossip centres – all rational substitutes for traditional patterns' (Jencks, 1991: 23). The aims of this architecture were profoundly humanitarian: citizens were to have all of their needs catered for in an organised manner that their traditional environments, the nineteenth-century industrial slums with poor sanitation and crumbling social infrastructures, had signally failed to provide. Despite these laudable aims, however, the effect of the massive programmes of industrial planning and construction that were undertaken by European and American governments was to force people into uniform landscapes that broke up traditional communities. People were asked to adapt to these rational schemes, but their failure to do so led frequently to the crime, vandalism and social isolation that pollute many of our modern-day housing developments.

For Jencks, this sort of development marks the culmination of the modernist movement in architecture, with its founding principles of rationality, universality and human engineering. People were just not as malleable as the International Style assumed. In contrast to this, post-modernist architectural design focuses on critical engagement with already existing spaces and styles, acknowledgement of regional identities and reference to local traditions. Through a process of what Jencks calls 'double coding', which appeals at once to elite and popular tastes, to the designers and the users, postmodernist architecture seeks to become eclectic by borrowing styles from different periods and 'quoting' aspects of other buildings in its designs. It thus, as Jencks argues, 'entails a return to the past as much as a movement forward. . . . These simultaneous returns are, however, tradition with a difference and that difference is the intervention of the modern world' (1987: 11). This is not, of course, simply a return to pre-modern architectural classicism. Rather, history is treated ironically with classical arches being reproduced in twisted steel or the flying buttresses of nearby churches being duplicated in glass as the covers for access escalators. The 'double code' both cites earlier traditions and acknowledges its contemporary context in the use of materials and design in order to create an environment that playfully refers to a range of styles and epochs to generate a multi-layered space for its inhabitants.

Another key writer on postmodern architecture, Kenneth Frampton, calls for a 'Critical Regionalism' (see Frampton, 1985), a form of architec-ture that resists the flattening out of difference that occurred in modernism by reasserting regional forms, traditions and materials. Examples of such playfully citational and regionally particular postmodern archi-tecture might include the architect Charles Moore's *Piazza d'Italia* in New Orleans, which reflects the Italian roots of the local community by parodying 'the Trevi fountain, Roman classical arches, even the geographical shape of the country itself, transcoding their historical forms into contemporary materials (neon, stainless steel) as befits a symbolic representation of Italian-American society' (Hutcheon, 2002: 12). One might also cite *Die Neue Staatsgalerie*, the State Art Gallery, in Stuttgart, Germany, which Jencks describes as 'the most impressive building of

Post-Modernism up to 1984', employing 'ironic representation and con-
textual response' (Jencks, 1987: 274) in its citations of classical Egyptian
and Roman cornices, arches and windows, and even presenting the car
park as a sort of ruined castle with holes in its walls and loose blocks
lying around its base. Deliberately 'arty' in its design and decoration, it
ironically responds to its high-art contents and context, and produces an
environment that is as open to aesthetic appreciation as the works it
contains.

Perhaps the most often cited example of postmodern architecture
is the Westin Bonaventure Hotel in Los Angeles. This building has been
discussed by a wide range of thinkers, most influentially the American
postmodern critic Fredric Jameson. Jameson sees it as aspiring to 'a total
space, a complete world, a miniature city' (1991: 40) in which new
types of interaction and congregation can occur. He claims that its 'great
reflective glass skin' and hard-to-find entrances lead to 'a peculiar and
placeless dissociation' in which the outside city is 'not even an exterior,
inasmuch as when you look at the hotel's outer walls you cannot see the
hotel itself but only the distorted image of everything that surrounds
it' (42). It is, he claims, a 'hyperspace' in which it is 'quite impossible to
get your bearings' (43) amongst the multiple floors with their continually
moving walkways, elevators, shopping complexes and gathering points.
The consequence of this, he argues, is intense disorientation or even a
schizophrenic experience of depthlessness (terms which will be discussed
in more detail in Chapter 5) that makes irrelevant the modes by which
traditional spaces have been experienced and mapped.

Postmodernism in architecture thus seeks to be a radicalisation of
modernism that employs its new materials but resists the uniformity and
state-organised social engineering on which the International Style was
based. Its often ironic citations of older styles do not, however, mark a
return to the pre-modern but instead quote pre-modern elements in
ways that both acknowledge the traditions from which the contemporary
springs and playfully reincorporate them into its futuristic designs. This is
not to say that the pre-modern has disappeared in today's society,
however. The slums of South-East Asia and the *barrios* of Latin America,
in which the destitute survive on the detritus of their rich city-dwelling
neighbours, are neither modernist nor postmodernist – although they
might, as we shall see, be a result of the economic organisation of post-

modern multinational capitalism. The goals of postmodern architectural theory are to humanise social environments rather than to transform their inhabitants to fit into pre-decided rational schemes while, at the same time, making the most of modern materials and advances in construction techniques. Whether or not such an enterprise has been, or can be, successful is, however, open to question, and will be discussed further as this book progresses.

MODERNISM AND POSTMODERNISM IN ART

If architectural postmodernism is marked by a refusal of the universality of the International Style and an ironic return to regional cultures and traditions, the distinction between modernism and postmodernism in art is much more complex. In his book, *Postmodernist Culture: An Introduction to Theories of the Contemporary*, Steven Connor notes of artistic modernism that, 'it would be theoretical suicide to try to deduce such a single stylistic norm from the work produced in painting and sculpture over 50 years and across three continents, in order to be able to locate a single modernist point of departure for postmodernism' (1997: 88). There is no International Style of modernist art and, as a consequence of this, artistic postmodernism is a much more divided and fragmentary field than architecture.

If there is anything that identifies a governing tendency amongst the diversity of modernist art, it is its propensity to set out to challenge established styles and forms. As has often been noted, artistic modernism is made up of a range of movements and formations that set out to overthrow any consensus that might exist within a given community about what art is and how it should represent the world. Each of these movements presented itself as an avant-garde, as a group of artists that came together to rewrite the rules of art. These formations include groups such as the Surrealists who integrated dream-imagery into their works to challenge the dominance of rationality, the Dadaists who aimed at similar ends by exploring nonsense and absurdity, the Futurists who sought to celebrate and represent the new technologies and their potential to transform human nature, as well as broader movements such as abstract expressionism which retreated from ideas of pictorial representation in order to experiment with the emotional impact of pure form and colour.

What can be grasped from this idea of avant-garde art is that for modernism a key purpose of art was to challenge and transform public ideas of what a work of art is. As the American philosopher and art critic Arthur C. Danto notes,

> The history of Modernism, beginning in the late 1880s, is a history of the dismantling of a concept of art which had been evolving for over half a millennium. Art did not have to be beautiful; it need make no effort to furnish the eye with an array of sensations equivalent to what the real world would furnish it with; need not have a pictorial subject; need not deploy its forms in a pictorial space; need not be the magical product of the artist's touch.
>
> (Danto, 1992: 4)

Each of the avant-garde movements set out in a different way to challenge expectations, shock and scandalise public taste and transform the ways in which the world could be represented. In order to show how these challenges work, I want to explore briefly two very different accounts of avant-garde modernism, each of which will imply very different post-modernist strains of art.

According to one of the most influential writers on modernist art, the American critic Clement Greenberg, the 'essence of Modernism lies . . . in the use of characteristic methods of a discipline to criticise the discipline itself, not in order to subvert it but in order to entrench it more firmly in its area of competence' (Greenberg, 1986–96: 4, 85). This notion picks up on the avant-garde idea of challenging the consensus about what art is, but gives it a specific rationale: the aim of modernism is to seek out the limits that define art in order to discover art's essential principles and differentiate it from other areas of culture. Publishing his essay 'Modernist Painting' in 1960, Greenberg is concerned to defend art from being 'levelled down' to what he calls 'entertainment' (1986–96: 4, 86), and he sees modernist experimentation as the key means of defining for art a separate domain. Each form of art, he argues, must seek to discover what is essential to it by stripping away all that is extraneous. Focusing specifically on painting, the essay asserts that 'the stressing of the ineluctable flatness of the surface' was the process by which 'pictorial art criticised and defined itself under Modernism' (1986–96: 4, 87). Modernism, in other words, sought to call the viewer's attention to the fact that what they were seeing was a work of art on a flat canvas. Unlike the painting that developed from the *Quattrocento* tradition – the style of art that emerged, as the name suggests, in Italy during the 1400s, which employed perspective to hide the flatness of the canvas and give a sense of the three-dimensionality of the subjects represented – modernist art made flatness a virtue by disrupting perspective and even moving away from realistic representation altogether. Through this process, art becomes increasingly abstract, as representation gives way to the sorts of formal experimentation one might find in Dutch artist Piet Mondrian's geometrical blocks of colour or the American painter Jackson Pollock's huge canvases covered with seemingly random drips and swirls of paint. In this sense, what defines modernism for Greenberg is that, whereas 'naturalistic art had dissembled the medium, using art to conceal art; Modernism uses art to call attention to art' (1986–96: 4, 86).

If Greenberg's analysis of modernism focuses exclusively on questions of definition and form, it is important not to forget that many modernist avant-garde theorists viewed art as a means of transforming the world itself. The French poet and critic André Breton, who wrote two manifestos that set out the aims of the avant-garde movement called Surrealism, captures the much more challenging and political aims of some European avant-garde groups in a statement from the 'First Manifesto of Surrealism', which was first published in 1924:

> Surrealism, such as I conceive of it, asserts our complete *non-conformism*. . . . The world is only very relatively in tune with thought, and incidents of this kind are only the most obvious episodes of a war in which I am proud to be participating. Surrealism is the 'invisible ray' which will one day enable us to overcome our opponents.
>
> (Breton, 1992: 438–9)

The ideas of 'non-conformism' and 'war', as well as the sense of disrupting established ideas of the world, were key to the aims of surrealist art. Through art, surrealism sought to undermine bourgeois culture, reason and identity, and to 'substitute itself for them in solving all the principal problems of life' (Breton, 1992: 438). The point was to shock, disturb and outrage the general public by producing art that would literally transform how the world was experienced. The idea that art can change the world might seem overly optimistic to many readers nowadays and yet, emerging out of the turmoil that overtook Europe during the first half of the twentieth century, it was a project undertaken by a whole series of avant-garde groups with the utmost rigour and seriousness. Thus the melting clocks in the paintings of Spanish artist Salvador Dali might seek to confront the spectator's views of the rigidity of time that organises their working lives, or German surrealist Hans Bellmer's deformed and mutated dolls might expose the implicit sexual sadism in traditional artistic representations of female beauty. The point of much surrealist art, according to Breton's manifestos, was not to be beautiful or moral but to challenge everyday conceptions about how the mind and the world worked: to shock its audience into questioning the assumptions that underpin their day-to-day beliefs.

If modernism in art was the age of the avant-gardes, then, for many critics, postmodernism marks the exhaustion of those projects, the end of a sense that art has a single purpose or can change the world, and yet it also indicates a democratisation of art coupled with a continuing expansion of the forms and techniques that might be counted as artistic as well as the involvement of sections of the community who had hitherto appeared to be marginal to the art world. As American critic Andreas Huyssen makes clear, a key aspect of postmodernism is the way in which it breaks down what he calls the 'Great Divide' between high art and popular culture (see Huyssen, 1986). Greenberg's argument that art should seek to define for itself a domain separate from popular culture and Breton's hatred of bourgeois society are rejected by many strands of postmodernism. So, for example, in the 'pop art' of American artists such as Roy Lichtenstein or Andy Warhol that began in the 1950s and caught the imagination of the mass media during the 1960s and 1970s, the commodities of the bourgeoisie are depicted in ways that are as much celebratory as they are critical. The former, Lichtenstein, reproduced frames from comic strips as huge oil paintings that ironically capture the stock images of American popular culture in all of their sentimentality and violence. Warhol, on the other hand, experimented with reproductions of a wide range of the objects of consumer culture, from soup cans to boxes of cleaning products and the faces of famous people including Marilyn Monroe and Richard Nixon. Pop art, and particularly Warhol's work, challenges the notion of a firm distinction between the supposedly rarefied sphere of serious high art and the commercial world of advertising in a way that sets the scene for many of the accounts of the culture of mass media manipulation that have come to be associated by critics with the postmodern.

If postmodernist art refuses the modernist distinction between the high and the popular, it retains a sense of art's mission to confront everyday beliefs and assumptions. In Europe, for example, the work of German artist Anselm Kiefer set out in the 1970s to explore the folklore and mythology of his country in order to reclaim some of the symbols of German identity from their manipulation by the Nazis during the 1930s. The 'Attic Paintings' that were first shown in 1973 borrow names and figures from the nationalist myths that had been employed to bolster Nazi ideology. However, they recontextualise these figures in ambiguous ways that challenge the spectator to question her or his relationship with both the near and the distant past, and that refuse to embrace the abstraction or minimalism associated with artistic modernism. In this series, the symbols of ancient German legends are disturbingly interwoven with allusions to a post-Second World War terrorist organisation, the Red Army Faction (see Kiefer, 2001: 36–47). This ambiguous use of mythical ideas and figures interspersed with problematic contemporary references presents an image of German history that refuses straightforward explanation and questions received notions of national identity and culture.

To give another example, during the 1980s female artists began to challenge the male-orientated balance of the art establishment. One particularly successful group, the Guerrilla Girls, named themselves 'The Conscience of the Art World' and used theatrical means to point out the under-representation of women in the major galleries. One piece, which began as a billboard poster but is now frequently reproduced as a work in its own right, is entitled 'Do women have to be naked to get into the Met. Museum?' and depicts a classical female nude wearing a gorilla mask next to the claim that 'Less than 5% of the *artists* in the Modern Art Sections are women, but 85% of the *nudes* are female.' Other artists such as the British duo Sarah Lucas and Tracey Emin use their work deliberately to parody masculine sexual repartee and thereby challenge the dominant constructions of gender identity that present men as voracious predators and women as their passive victims.

If the experimentation of these artists extends the scope of what art can be and introduces new voices and styles into the galleries, it is also seen by some critics as a loss of critical edge as art embraces the markets and, apart from some minor scandals which often serve only to increase a work's popularity, is embraced in its turn by the very bourgeoisie against whom modernism set itself up in opposition. Kiefer, Lucas and Emin might have caused some brief scandals, but their work has quickly become as marketable as that of the modernists whom they succeeded. It is perhaps not just a coincidence that the 1980s saw the fastest growing art market in history: art and finance seem to some critics to be becoming more and more closely related as the distinctions between high and popular culture disappear and artists become mass-media stars in their own right.

READING THE POSTMODERN TEXT: POSTMODERNISM AND LITERATURE

According to the British critic Tim Woods,

> It is in the field of literary studies that the term 'postmodernism' has received the widest usage and provoked the most intense debate. There have been many attempts to theorise the consequences and mani-festations of postmodernism for literature, all usually running into problems of historical and formal definition.
>
> (Woods, 1999: 49)

As Woods suggests, literary postmodernism is a many-faceted formation that has led to a good deal of 'vexed debate' between critics, and so, rather than attempting to sum up what it is all about in a short section, a close reading of a particular work will be used to introduce some of the most influential theories of literary postmodernism, ones that will come into play in further discussions of literature later in this book. Thus, while the last two sections have introduced postmodern architecture and art by focusing on the ideas and categories produced by theorists and illustrating them with examples of practice, in looking at postmodernism in literature I want to focus instead on a particular work and move on to investigate the ways in which some influential critics might approach it. The text chosen for this, the Scottish author Alasdair Gray's 1992 novel *Poor Things*, is, by any reasonable account, postmodern. After a brief outline of the novel's plot and structure, I shall describe how three critics of post-modern literature, Brian McHale, Fredric Jameson and Linda Hutcheon, might analyse its style and impact.

Set in nineteenth-century Scotland, *Poor Things* is a parodic rewriting of Mary Shelley's *Frankenstein*, in which the male monster is replaced by a sexually voracious woman created by a doctor, Godwin Bysshe Baxter, who places the brain of a foetus within the body of its drowned mother to save the lives of both. Baxter, whose full name evokes both Mary Shelley's father, William Godwin, and her husband, Percy Bysshe Shelley, is himself a strangely inhuman, mechanical presence, and with his huge size, high-pitched voice, bizarre eating habits and need for sustaining medicines is much more the monster than she. What seems to be the central narrative of the novel charts their relationship through to her marriage and his death.

Escaping from her creator with a sleazy lawyer, Bella, the female pro-tagonist, embarks upon an odyssey through nineteenth-century Europe. She meets a range of different figures, some of whom are fictional while others, such as the psychologist Jean Martin Charcot, are not. The story is told by a number of means such as letters and diaries that have been collected together and fleshed out by Bella's eventual husband, a doctor called Archibald McCandless. His manuscript was later published in only one copy, but never distributed, and is discovered by the book's narrator, 'Alasdair Gray'. This is not the full extent of the novel, however. Along with McCandless's narrative it includes a letter from one Victoria McCandless, his 'real-life' wife and the model for Bella, stating that none of it is true, and that the book only emerged from the deluded ravings of her jealous husband. As well as this letter, there is also an introduction by 'Gray' describing how the manuscript was found and eventually lost again, and a long series of scholarly footnotes written by 'Gray' and a local historian to prove the truth of the events described. Nothing in this book is as it seems: the reviews printed before the title page are a mixture of largely positive quotations from 'real' papers such as *The Scotsman*, *The Independent* and *The Sunday Telegraph*, and rather damning ones from a number of strange fictitious publications including *Private Nose* and *The*

Times Literary Implement. From even this brief account, it should be clear that the text of *Poor Things* is irreducibly plural, made up as it is of a range of competing voices and styles, and fragmentary in that these voices do not form a coherent whole but continually contradict and undermine each other.

This is the aspect of postmodern fiction that the American critic Brian McHale introduces in his book, *Postmodernist Fiction* (1987). McHale argues that the move from modern to postmodern fiction is marked by a change from a focus on epistemological issues to an exploration of ontological questions. By this he means that modern fiction asks about how a world can be interpreted or changed, and is interested in questions of truth and knowledge, i.e. in epistemology. The simplest example of this is the literary detective who sifts the evidence presented in order to discover who committed the crime. Postmodern fiction, on the other hand, raises questions about the very status of reality and the world: 'What is a world?; What kinds of world are there, how are they constituted, and how do they differ?; What happens when different kinds of world are placed in confrontation, or when boundaries between worlds are violated?' (McHale, 1987: 10). In other words, according to McHale postmodern fiction confronts the reader with questions about what sort of world is being created at each moment in the text, and who or what in a text they can believe or rely on, i.e. questions of ontology. In the case of *Poor Things*, the conflict between the fantastical story told by McCandless and his wife's far more mundane account of the same events presented through the lens of nineteenth-century medicine generates a range of questions about what is real and what might really be going on. Moreover, the scholarly footnotes that try to prove the reality of some of the more outlandish elements of the story and the conflict between 'Gray' and the local historian – the former believes McCandless has written a 'true history' and the latter thinks it is an imaginative fiction – force the reader to engage in what McHale calls 'a suspension of belief as well as disbelief' (1987: 33). We are never certain what to take as true or untrue, as the seeming plausibility of Victoria's narrative is continually challenged by the fact that Archibald's is so much more interesting and enticing and has the support of the novel's narrator who, traditionally, might be expected to be at least vaguely trustworthy. Even the reviews printed before the title page produce a bizarre movement between the 'real world' and its fictional counterpart that unsettles any firm or fixed boundaries one might wish to erect between the two. On this reading, then, *Poor Things* develops as a postmodern narrative by placing its readers in a state of continual ontological uncertainty.

This uncertainty about the reality of the fictional world is more than just artistic playfulness. It provides a means by which the work of fiction can engage with cultural and political questions, a point that is picked up by both Jameson and the Canadian postmodernist critic Linda Hutcheon. In his hugely influential book, *Postmodernism, or, the Cultural Logic of Late Capitalism* (1991), Jameson provides an analysis of postmodern literature that focuses on its broader cultural and political import. He argues that the advent of postmodernity marks a 'new depthlessness', a 'consequent weakening of historicity' and a 'schizophrenic' subjectivity (1991: 6). These categories will all be examined in more detail during the discussion of Jameson's arguments about the politics of postmodern culture in Chapter 5. What is important to grasp here, however, is how Jameson describes their effect on literature. In the face of today's mass-media society, he argues, postmodern literature offers little scope for resistance: the distinction between high art and popular culture has been effaced by the commodification of artistic production, and the critical thrust of modern parody has become nothing more than blank mimicry with a pastiche that is 'amputated of the satiric impulse' and 'devoid of laughter' (1991: 17). Parody, according to Jameson, has a critical edge: it challenges and subverts that which it mimics. Pastiche, on the other hand, is concerned only with the superficial appropriation of different modes and genres for the generation of its own performative style. *Poor Things* certainly has the range of sources that Jameson identifies with pastiche: besides *Frankenstein*, it draws on Shakespeare, Edgar Allan Poe, Charles Dickens, Walter Scott and Lewis Carroll, as well as Henry Gray's nineteenth-century study of the human body, *Anatomy*, from which pictures are taken for inclusion in the text. The novel moves rapidly between high and popular culture, and deliberately subverts the distinction by producing a cartoon version of the *Mona Lisa* and describing *Hamlet* as a tragedy brought about by a form of madness that developed in the Danish court as a result of its unsanitary sewerage system. What is less clear, however, is whether this means that the book lacks any critical edge.

While a Jameson-style critique seems likely to read *Poor Things* as a playful abdication from political engagement, an approach based on the work of Hutcheon might be more open to its potential to raise important questions about social issues and problems. In *The Poetics of Postmodernism*, Hutcheon argues that the literary techniques that make the postmodern such a 'contradictory cultural enterprise' (1988: 106) come together to form a genre she calls 'historiographic metafiction'. This is a self-conscious mode of writing, a writing that 'meta-fictionally' comments on and investigates its own status as fiction as well as questioning our ideas of the relation between fiction, reality and truth. Its focus on history opens up problems about the possibility of access to a 'true' past as a way of de-naturalising present ideas and institutions. Hutcheon argues that whereas the traditional form of historical fiction 'incorporates and assimilates' data from the past 'in order to lend a feeling of verifiability' to the text, historiographic metafiction 'incorporates, but rarely assimilates such data' and thereby 'acknowledges the paradox of the *reality* of the past but its *textualised accessibility* to us today' (1988: 114). This directly challenges Jameson's notion of the loss of historical perspective. For Hutcheon, there is no question that the past is real; what is at stake is the access that we are able to have to it and the effects it can have on contemporary ideas and actions. She argues that postmodern fiction depicts the past as a series of problematic and often contradictory texts, events and artefacts that confront the reader, thereby giving rise to a series of complex questions about 'identity and subjectivity; the question of reference and representation; the intertextual nature of the past; and the ideological implications of writing about history' (1988: 117). Again, these structural questions about the processes of narration are key to *Poor Things*: the problem of the identity of Bella/Victoria is never resolved, nor is the issue of whether Archibald or Victoria is telling the truth. Nineteenth-century Europe is presented by all of the voices in the book in terms of a series of overlapping literary, popular fictional, artistic and historical texts: the reader is never short of intertexts to recognise – which is, of course, the stuff of Jameson's pastiche – and never knows which tells the truth. And finally, the novel's numerous interactions with various political formations from the period, from anarchism or liberalism to imperialism or socialism, continually raise questions about how best to grasp the present as a consequence of these past conflicts. If for Jameson, then, postmodernism marks an abdication from political responsibility, engagement and critique, for Hutcheon it opens new political channels to challenge the dominant ideological discourses of the present. As this book progresses, these two positions on literary postmodernism will be explored in more detail to show how they relate to questions of identity, history and politics.

POSTMODERNISM AS IMMANENT CRITIQUE

The discussion of *Poor Things* raises another important question about postmodernism: if Gray's is a postmodern novel, what might we make of *Frankenstein? Poor Things* throws up all of the problems about the politics of representation mentioned above, but doesn't *Frankenstein* raise similar and equally complex questions? Of course it is a very different, less outrageously funny, novel, but it is important not to forget that its literary form is not simply that of a 'straightforward' or 'realist' (whatever these terms might mean) narrative. *Frankenstein* itself employs many of the techniques, such as frame narratives, ontological indeterminacy and unreliable narrators, that were identified as crucial to the postmodernism of *Poor Things*. What should we make of this? Might *Frankenstein* too be described as, in some sense, postmodern?

This idea seems to fly in the face of a common but rather crude understanding of the relation between history and artistic representation that is often associated with postmodernism. One critical commonplace has it that the history of the novel can be split into three phases, and there are similar versions of this argument for other literary genres as well as architecture, art and many other cultural and media forms. The first phase is realism, which begins in the eighteenth century with the work of authors such as Daniel Defoe and Samuel Richardson, and aims to present as lifelike an image of the world as possible by masking the conventional character of its construction. This is followed by the modernism of the late nineteenth and early twentieth centuries, which tends to be represented by the work of writers such as Virginia Woolf and James Joyce, and is deliberately difficult and elitist in its experimentations that aim to explore life and experience differently. Third and finally comes postmodernism, exemplified by the work of such authors as John Barth, Salman Rushdie or Alasdair Gray, which continues formally to experiment with literary technique but refuses to take up the elitist stance of the modernists and instead prefers to play with popular cultural reference and pastiche. From this perspective, the relationship between realism, modernism and postmodernism is seen as a gradual progress from the restrictions of the first to the freedom and experimentation of the last.

In contrast to this account, there is a range of critics who argue persuasively that postmodernism can be located throughout literary history (for particularly astute examples of this see Elam (1992) and Readings and Schaber (1993)), and that *Frankenstein* might therefore be just as postmodern as *Poor Things*. If postmodernism is thought of as a style rather than a period, there should certainly be no question but that texts and works of art from earlier times might be considered postmodern if they employ the range of formal devices associated with postmodernism. Alongside *Frankenstein*, literary texts that have been identified most frequently as stylistically if not historically postmodern include Cervantes' *Don Quixote* (1604–14), Laurence Sterne's *Tristram Shandy* (1759–67) Lewis Carroll's *Alice* books (1865 and 1872) and James Joyce's *Ulysses* (1922) and *Finnegans Wake* (1939). Each of these texts employs many of the formal techniques identified by McHale, Jameson and Hutcheon in the last section, even though all of them were written earlier than what tends to be recognised as the era of postmodernism.

Critics who argue for a stylistic rather than period-based account of postmodernism tend to follow the arguments about artistic representation developed by the French philosopher Jean-François Lyotard in his essay 'An Answer to the Question, What is the Postmodern?' (1992: 1–16). In this essay, Lyotard continues to employ the terms realism, modernism and postmodernism, and yet he does so in a way that rejects the sense of historical periodisation that has just been outlined. All three coexist simultaneously in any culture and indicate different modes of presentation within a given milieu. Realism, he argues, is the mainstream style of a culture, and its task is to depict the world 'from a point of view that would give it a recognisable meaning' in order that its audience can 'decode images and sequences rapidly' and thereby 'protect [their] consciousness from doubt' (1992: 5–6). In other words, its aim is to depict the world according to conventions with which the reader or viewer is already familiar so that it can quickly and unproblematically be understood. This sort of realism might certainly apply to the form of narrative employed in many nineteenth-century novels, but it can also be found in contemporary phenomena, such as Hollywood film, popular music and advertising, that follow recognisably established patterns.

In contrast to realism, Lyotard sets modernism and postmodernism, both of which he sees as potentially disruptive forms whose task is, he says, 'presenting the existence of something unpresentable. Showing that there is something we can conceive of that we can neither see nor show' (1992: 11). What he means by this is that rather than reproducing what is immediately recognisable, modern and postmodern works of art disrupt recognition by alluding to what a particular culture represses or excludes from its normal means of communication. They are, in other words, deliberately difficult and disturbing, challenging accepted practices of presentation and understanding. Lyotard, invoking the categories of philosophical aesthetics, calls the effect of this sort of art 'sublime'. In contrast to the beautiful, which is based on a feeling of harmony and attraction between the subject and the work, the sublime indicates a mixed feeling of pleasure and pain: simultaneous attraction and repulsion, awe and terror. It disturbs, and challenges the subject to respond without determining in advance what form that response should take. This notion of the sublime as a disturbance of everyday sense-making activity is, as will become apparent as the book progresses, central to postmodern theory, whether it is dealing with art, technology or politics.

Lyotard distinguishes between the modern and the postmodern sublime by arguing that in the former the unpresentable is 'invoked only as absent content, while the form, thanks to its recognisable consistency, continues to offer the reader material for consolation or pleasure' (1992: 14), while the latter 'invokes the unpresentable in presentation itself' (1992: 15). In other words, modern art presents the fact that there is within the culture in which it exists something that eludes presentation but does so in a form that remains familiar to the reader or viewer. So, to cite Lyotard's own example, the French novelist Marcel Proust's *A la recherche du temps perdu*, translated into English as both *In Search of Lost Time* and *Remembrance of Things Past*, depicts a narrator/protagonist whose psychological transformations over time are impossible to present within the conventional narrative form it employs, and yet are alluded to as the 'absent content' of that text. The form of the novel is recognisable here, but its content disturbs because of the allusions that it continually makes to a sense of a relation between time and identity that cannot be pinned down by conventional narrative or psychological criteria.

In contrast to this modernist sublime, postmodernism confronts the reader or viewer with a work that is challenging in terms of both form and content. Lyotard mentions the Irish writer James Joyce here, arguing that his last works, *Ulysses* and *Finnegans Wake*, which employ puns, obscure allusions, quotations and a whole range of means to disrupt readers' perceptions about what a novel should be, generate 'new presentations – not to take pleasure in them, but to better produce the feeling that there is something unpresentable' (1992: 15). Each text explodes the traditional form of the novel, disturbing the reader and disrupting normal processes of understanding through both their content and structure.

The modern and the postmodern are presented here as dynamic forms that work to disrupt the expectations of a culture, and change as that culture is transformed and readers and spectators become used to, and no longer shocked by, their contents and methods. In this sense they are comparable to the avant-gardes discussed earlier in terms of modernist art, which set out deliberately to challenge and disturb. For Lyotard, the role of postmodernism is thus to perform an immanent critique of the day-to-day structures of realism. What this means is that it operates within the realist context of a given culture to shatter its norms and challenge its assumptions, not with a new set of criteria drawn from outside of that culture, but rather by showing the contradictions the culture contains, what it represses, refuses to recognise or makes unpresentable. In other words, according to Lyotard:

> The postmodern artist or writer is in the position of a philosopher: the text he writes or the work he creates is not in principle governed by preestablished rules and cannot be judged . . . by the application of given categories to this text or work. Such rules and categories are what the work or text is investigating.
>
> (1992: 15)

Postmodernism breaks the rules of both form and content, calling for a transformation of critical assumptions as a culture attempts to respond to the immanent critique of those categories and laws.

This model of postmodernism presents culture as a continually mutating entity that is made up of a series of challenges and readjustments as postmodern works are assimilated. In other words, what counts as modernism or postmodernism will change as a culture adapts to the provocations that works of art produce. Equally, works that are post-modern for one culture may be modern or even realist for another. As Lyotard argues, a work of art 'can become modern only if it is first postmodern. Thus understood, postmodernism is not modernism at its end, but in a nascent state, and this state is recurrent' (1992: 13). Thus, for example, Marcel Duchamp's work *The Fountain* (1917), which comprised a urinal laid on its back and signed with the name 'R. Mutt', might have originated as postmodern because of the way in which it challenged the rules of what a work of art could be, but now that it is shown in galleries and accepted as art it ceases to have the shock value it once had and can be appreciated, 'understood' and reconciled with contemporary ideas of artistic form much more immediately.

POSTMODERNISM AND POSTMODERNITY

These sketches of the different versions of postmodernism are merely a starting point, and must be developed if a proper grasp of what is at stake in the postmodern is to be attained. A discussion that focuses entirely on the stylistic features of postmodernist culture without investigating the social, economic and political contexts from which it emerges is too crude an undertaking to be particularly helpful to any serious critic of either postmodernism or postmodernity. It implies, for a start, that artistic style can be divorced from its historical and political contexts: that works of contemporary art, architecture, literature or culture can somehow be separated from the radical transformations taking place in the world at present, and that artistic experimentation can turn its back on reality to become tied up only with self-reflexive questions of form. As Jameson argues, however, the postmodern 'is not just another word for the description of a particular style. It is also . . . a periodising concept whose function is to correlate the emergence of new formal features in culture with the emergence of a new type of social life and a new economic order' (1983: 113). Hutcheon's ideas of historiographical metafiction also refer frequently to the technological and political transformations that have occurred since the 1960s. Even Lyotard's formalist analysis of the relations between realism, modernism and postmodernism necessarily makes reference to a notion of historical context in terms of the idea that cultures have particular realist ways of depicting the world that are open to challenge and transformation.

Given only a moment's consideration, it should be clear that the simplistic separation of style and context is unworkable: whether it is postmodern or not, artistic work emerges from the world in which it occurs, engages with and comments upon the way things are, and presents alternatives to them. Even the most apparently bizarre and experimental work of contemporary art or literature responds to the general culture in some way or other, even if it is by rejecting entirely its values and associations. Equally, architectural style is inextricable from economic factors such as who is to pay for the construction of new buildings and who can afford to buy or rent them. It is no coincidence, for instance, that the emergence of postmodern architecture coincided with the collapse of the vast state-sponsored building programmes of the immediate post-war regeneration of Europe. Nowadays architects must appeal to private companies with their desires to project their corporate identities through their built environments, and uniformity and universalism have fallen rapidly from grace.

If one wishes to understand postmodernism at any more than the superficial level of contemporary cultural fashion, it is important to explore its relationship with the wider social and political 'periodising concept' of postmodernity. What needs to be investigated in terms of the postmodern is the series of questions raised about how the various postmodernist styles connect with and present the different social, political and historical postmodernities, and to do that one must first have a clear sense of what is meant by such terms as 'modernity' and 'postmodernity'.

2

MODERNITY AND POSTMODERNITY

One of the earliest uses of the term 'postmodernity' occurs in Arnold Toynbee's *A Study of History*, published in 1954. Here he defines post-modernity as a historical epoch beginning in the final quarter of the nineteenth century and marking a period of almost continual strife that has persisted ever since: 'A post-Modern Age of Western history', he argues, sees 'the rhythm of a Modern Western war-and-peace broken . . . by the portent of one general war following hard on the heels of another' (Toynbee, 1954: 235). This epoch comes at the end of a long and steady progress during which humanity has moved from the 'Dark Ages' (675–1075), through the 'Middle Ages' (1075–1475) to the 'Modern Age' (1475–1875). The modern, according to Toynbee, is the period that saw the rise of 'humanism', which understands the world in terms of a recognition that human beings are the basis of knowledge and action, are inherently valuable and dignified, and have free will. It is the epoch of gradual emancipation from superstition and mysticism as the Enlight-enment, which became central to philosophical thought during the seventeenth and eighteenth centuries, sought to provide a rational and scientific basis for human experience. If the modern is the zenith of progress and development, then, for Toynbee, postmodernity is a period of decline in which wars rage incessantly and the humanist projects of the

Enlightenment are abandoned in the nationalist conflicts that marred much of the first half of the twentieth century. Presenting postmodernity as a period of crisis and linking it with the decline of humanist and Enlightenment values is, as we shall see, a common and often persuasive gesture, and, as Stuart Sim argues, 'in Toynbee we have a vision of postmodernity as a journey into unknown territory where the old cultural constraints no longer apply, and our collective security is potentially compromised' (2002: 17). Since Toynbee's intervention in 1954, a wide range of critics have adopted the term and developed their own much more detailed analyses of the cultural, political, philosophical and historical stakes of postmodernity. Toynbee's identification of postmodernity as a predominantly twentieth-century phenomenon is, however, one that most of these accounts support.

Many of the different ideas and perspectives about postmodernism and postmodernity that have been mentioned or discussed so far in this book develop, albeit in significantly different ways, from the notion that a series of fundamental transformations took place in the world during the twentieth century, and particularly in the period following the Second World War. According to these accounts, postmodernity is a social formation that takes root in the last years of the nineteenth century, puts forth its first shoots amid the social, economic and military conflicts that scarred the first half of the twentieth, and comes into its own about the middle of that century as it replaces the modern as the dominant form of cultural and social organisation. Trends such as globalisation, the transformations of colonial power, the development of new media and communication networks, and the collapse of religious and political traditions and beliefs across the world all appear to point towards a culture that has rapidly become fundamentally different from that experienced by earlier generations. The threat of the obliteration of all existence, whether brought about by nuclear war or natural catastrophe, has weighed on ideas of what it is to be part of a community or society, and even what it is to be human, forcing thoroughgoing reconceptualisations of some of the most basic categories of philosophical, social and political thought. In the light of these threats, the question that seems most to trouble the apocalyptic imaginings of some recent commentators is whether the world will end in fire or ice: the atomic firestorm or the nuclear winter, global warming or the slow freezing of the universe in entropic 'heat death'.

Steven Best and Douglas Kellner argue that these changes are 'comparable in scope to the shifts produced by the Industrial Revolution', and that, as the world enters 'the Third Millennium, we are thus witnessing the advent of a digitised and networked global economy and society, fraught with promise and danger' (2001: 1). The modern world, and the certainties and projects that went along with it, has, according to Best and Kellner, fractured and is now open to new forces, possibilities and threats, in the form of those ideas grouped together under the title 'postmodern'. The result of this, for some critics, is that what the postmodern serves to promote is 'a sceptical ethos which simply takes for granted the collapse of all realist or representationalist paradigms . . . and the need henceforth to abandon any thought of criticising social injustice from a standpoint of class solidarity' (Norris, 1993: 23). For others, however, it marks a point at which a 'proliferation of discursive interventions and arguments' can occur, and it thus 'becomes a source of a greater activism and a more radical libertarianism' as postmodern theory 'further radicalises the emancipatory possibilities offered by the Enlightenment and Marxism' (Laclau, 1988: 79–80). Equally, as the last chapter attempted to show, postmodernist art and culture also appear to have come to supplant modernism, challenging some of its preconceptions and transforming its procedures. The distinctions between high art and popular culture as well as ruling ideas of critical orthodoxy and aesthetic value have fallen into disrepute. For some postmodernist critics, this leads to new forms of critical practice that are able to analyse art with different goals and categories, freed at last from the old systems and rules of taste and judgement. For other critics who are less persuaded of the efficacy of postmodern thought, the loss of these systems of taste removes any criteria for distinguishing the good from the bad, the progressive from the reactionary, and leaves us with a culture in which 'anything goes' so long as it is capable of generating profit.

Before passing judgement on whether the postmodern is a positive or negative formation, it is important to continue to establish a sense of how it has been identified by its supporters and detractors. To do this, this chapter will introduce the work of two key thinkers of modernity and postmodernity: the first, Jean-François Lyotard, defines postmodernity as the contemporary condition in which we live and champions postmodern forms of resistance and criticism, and the second, the German philosopher Jürgen Habermas, provides an account of modernity that seeks to defend its projects and practices as still being crucial to critique and politics today.

THE POSTMODERN CONDITION:
JEAN-FRANÇOIS LYOTARD

Lyotard's book, *The Postmodern Condition: A Report on Knowledge*, first published in 1979, has come to stand for many critics as one of the most comprehensive and influential accounts of postmodernity. Unlike the argument in his essay 'An Answer to the Question, What is the Postmodern?', which was written some three years later, he here sets out to identify the contemporary world as postmodern. As the book's subtitle suggests, what it investigates is the 'condition of knowledge in the most highly developed societies' (1984: xxiii). This includes discussions of what counts as knowledge for us today, how it is generated, communicated and put to use by individuals, businesses and whole societies. The hypothesis behind Lyotard's argument is that 'the status of knowledge is altered as societies enter what is known as the postindustrial age and cultures enter what is known as the postmodern age' (1984: 3). Crucial to this is the question of ownership: who controls the flow of ideas and who has access to them. We now live, he argues, in a knowledge-driven economy in which technological innovation and the ability to access and manipulate ideas rapidly is a key means of surviving, flourishing and making profits. As a result, we become consumers of a knowledge that has been transformed into a commodity: 'Knowledge is and will be produced in order to be sold, it is and will be consumed in order to be valorised in a new production: in both cases, the goal is exchange' (1984: 4). This commercially based view of knowledge marks, for Lyotard, a significant shift away from the ways in which knowledge was conceived by earlier generations, and particularly during modernity.

To highlight the differences between modern forms of knowing and the ways in which contemporary ideas are generated and communicated, Lyotard analyses knowledge in terms of narratives: the ways in which the world is understood through the stories we tell about it – which include everything from particle physics to magazine gossip columns – that tie together disparate ideas, impressions and events to form coherent sequences. This is not to imply that physics is the equivalent of gossip or that all knowledge is akin to fiction, but, rather, that our understanding of the world is made up of the numerous different ways in which we discuss and experience it. So, for example, history tells stories of the past, psychology chronicles the structures of experience, and science generates narratives that explain the workings of the natural world. Each of these forms of narrative is grounded in a particular set of rules and procedures, which might be explicit or implicit, so that, for example, there are clear rules for what counts as a legitimate scientific argument, but what we would think of as good or bad gossip is much harder to specify according to a system of laws. Lyotard calls the sets of rules that determine the legitimacy of particular forms of narrative 'metanarratives', and argues that these metanarratives provide criteria that allow one to judge which ideas and statements are legitimate, true and ethical for each different form of narrative. So, for example, the phrase 'My love is like a red, red rose' might be highly evocative within the discourse of poetry because of its suggestive and symbolic qualities, but would be likely to be considered illegitimate as a description of a particular type of flower in botany as it flaunts the rules of experimental verification and classification according to genus and species.

Alongside metanarratives that legitimate individual ideas and statements, Lyotard also introduces the concept of the grand narrative. Grand narratives are, for Lyotard, the governing principles of modernity, and it is through his analyses of them that he defines modernity and illustrates how it has given way to a postmodern condition. Bringing together all of the different narrative and metanarrative forms of a particular culture, grand narratives produce systematic accounts of how the world works, how it develops over history, and the place of human beings within it. Put simply, grand narratives construct accounts of human society and progress. In *The Postmodern Condition* Lyotard identifies two main forms of grand narrative: speculation and emancipation. The former, the speculative grand narrative, charts progress through the development of knowledge as individual ideas and discoveries build towards a systematic whole that reveals the truth of human existence under the auspices of a particular metanarrative: for the speculative grand narrative, 'True knowledge . . . is comprised of reported statements [that] are incorporated into a metanarrative of a subject that guarantees their legitimacy'

(1984: 35). In other words, the speculative grand narrative charts the progress and development of knowledge towards a systematic truth: a grand unified theory in which our place in the universe will be understood. The grand narrative of emancipation, on the other hand, sees the development of knowledge as driving human freedom as it emancipates humanity from mysticism and dogma through education: knowledge, on this account, 'is no longer the subject, but in the service of the subject' (1984: 36). The point here is that the development of knowledge is seen as a tool to improve the human condition, help people to understand their place in the world and emancipate them from prejudice, oppression and ignorance. By tying together all of the different narratives and metanarratives that make up a culture, assigning values to them and giving them a goal, modernity's grand narratives present an idea of the development of knowledge as a progress towards universal enlightenment and freedom.

With the move towards the postmodern, however, Lyotard argues that the nature and status of knowledge change. He sees the recent transformations in capitalism and the political systems that accompany them as shattering the systematic or emancipatory aims of the grand narrative: 'the project of modernity', he argues, 'has not been forsaken or forgotten, but destroyed, "liquidated"' (1992: 18). The loss of overarching grand narratives and their ideas of progress means that the structures that legitimate knowledge, the metanarratives, also begin to lose their power and stability. This leads to Lyotard's most often cited argument: 'I define *postmodern* as incredulity toward metanarratives' (1984: xxiv). By this he means that the criteria that organise knowledge, sort the legitimate from the illegitimate in each discipline and guide the development of thought are no longer as persuasive as they were when they formed a part of a modern grand narrative. He argues that the criteria of universalism and emancipation have been replaced by a single criterion: profit. Contemporary capitalism, he argues, 'does not constitute a universal history, it is trying to constitute a world market' (1988: 179). The difference here is the way that particular pieces of narrative (phrases, in the language Lyotard uses here) are held together: 'capital's superiority over the speculative [grand narrative] resides at least in its not seeking to have the last word, to totalise after the fact all the phrases that have taken place . . . but rather in seeking to have the next word' (1988: 138). In other words, while the grand narratives seek to draw all knowledge into a single system, capitalism is more than happy with fragmentation, so long as those fragments of knowledge continue to develop, grow and make a profit. The postmodern condition is thus one in which the demands of capitalist economics rule supreme, and all developments of knowledge are determined by the pragmatic logic of the markets rather than the overarching dream of a universal human good.

Lyotard argues that knowledge has itself become a commodity, and that it is also the basis of power: 'Knowledge in the form of an informational commodity indispensable to productive power is already, and will continue to be, a major – perhaps *the* major – stake in the worldwide competition for power' (1984: 5). The most powerful people and societies are the ones who have the greatest knowledge resources: those with the best technology, the most advanced communications and weapons systems, the most highly developed medicines and the means to collect the most detailed information about their competitors. Research and development are funded by businesses and governments to give them a competitive edge in the world markets. The global competition for power, according to Lyotard, has thus become a battle for knowledge, and the goal is efficiency. As a result of this transformation, he describes the imperative of contemporary culture in stark terms, arguing that capitalism 'necessarily entails a certain level of terror: be operational . . . or disappear' (1984: xxiv). The sole criterion for judging the worth of a narrative is its efficacy in making the capitalist system work more quickly and more efficiently. The effects of this operational criterion can be seen throughout much of contemporary society, frequently surfacing in arguments that define education almost solely as a means of producing the skills that improve the competitiveness of the workforce, and the arts as primarily a sector that contributes towards the health of the economy. Other criteria of justification are, he claims, gradually being eclipsed.

In the light of this, Lyotard sees the main threat facing members of a postmodern society as the reduction of all knowledge to a system whose only criterion is efficiency. He argues that in the contemporary world the markets for science and technology, having lost touch with the emancipatory goals of the modern grand narratives, have come to form 'a vanguard machine dragging humanity after it, dehumanising it' (1984: 63) as all forms of knowledge begin to be judged solely in terms of their

financial value and technological efficacy. The financial markets determine the value of everything, even human life, and any sense that there
are emancipatory goals for the modern grand narratives is coming to be
regarded with more and more 'incredulity':

> The question (overt or implied) now asked by the professionalist
> student, the State, or institutions of higher education is no longer 'Is it
> true?' but 'What use is it?' In the context of the mercantilisation of
> knowledge, more often than not this question is equivalent to: 'Is it
> saleable?' And in the context of power-growth: 'Is it efficient?' . . . What
> no longer makes the grade is competence as defined by other criteria
> true/false, just/unjust, etc.
>
> (Lyotard, 1984: 51)

If the grand narratives of modernity are premised upon the development
towards truth and justice, their obsolescence marks a condition in which
pragmatism takes over from ethics and the calculation of efficiency and
profit takes over as the driving force of action.

A wide range of thinkers has questioned *The Postmodern Condition*'s
analysis of contemporary knowledge. In a particularly pertinent challenge, the British critic Steven Connor takes Lyotard's account of the
postmodern to task on the basis of his analysis of metanarratives, particularly in relation to science: he argues that although scientific research
'is increasingly subject to the consideration of immediate use and profit-
ability' this does not necessarily lead to the breakdown of consensus or the
fragmentation of scientific discourse; in fact, a key strain of contemporary
research aims at 'the construction of unifying theories to account for the
operation of all the forces known in nature – a grand narrative if ever
there was one' (Connor, 1997: 30–1). In other words, *The Postmodern
Condition*, he argues, places too much stress on the fragmentation of
science's grand narratives without accounting for the persistence of those
very narratives in contemporary scientific research.

This critique might be generalised to question the notion of a general
breakdown of consensus in the postmodern world, which seems a
particularly vexed point in contemporary political thought. Lyotard's
account of postmodern culture anticipates many of the arguments put
forward by contemporary campaigners about the effects of globalisation

(see, for example, Burbach, 2001, Klein, 2000, Monbiot, 2000, 2003, or Stiglitz, 2002 for popular and straightforward analyses of this) in that it anticipates their analyses of the consequences of the commodification of international politics. It does not, however, leave space for the reassertion of grand narrative politics that has come to the fore during the twenty-first century in the so-called 'War on Terrorism' undertaken by George W. Bush, Tony Blair and their allies: one only has to remember that the names given to the second Gulf War by US planners were 'Operation Infinite Justice' and then, when that was recognised to be offensive to Muslims who equate such ideas only with the will of Allah, 'Operation Enduring Freedom' to see that there are still some who cling to at least the rhetoric of modern grand narrative organisation. More generally, the increased fragmentation of Western societies has, in recent years, gone hand in hand with the growing influence of fundamentalist religious beliefs in both the developing and developed world that resist entirely not just the postmodern but also the enlightenment rationalism of the scientifically based discourses of the modern. If these strains and tensions are to be grasped, a more nuanced notion of postmodernity and its relation to the modern must be developed.

Contemporary culture, it would seem, has not simply broken with modernity, but presents the critic with a much more complex formation. Lyotard's analysis of the postmodern commercialisation of knowledge has a good deal of force and is certainly recognisable in today's market-driven world, but one must be careful to recognise the persistence of the modern, or even the pre-modern, in many aspects of politics and culture today. A compelling analysis of postmodernity must be able to account for this tension, and must therefore be able to engage with the modern in a sophisticated manner. This is not a matter of simply rejecting the arguments of *The Postmodern Condition*, but rather of complementing Lyotard's discussions in that book with a more nuanced description of the relation between the modern and the postmodern that is capable of examining the persistence of aspects of the former in the latter.

THE MEANING OF 'POST-'

In many of the postmodernisms and postmodernities introduced so far, the prefix 'post-' has designated a process of historical succession in which the postmodern follows on from and replaces the modern. 'Post-' in these cases seems, quite simply, to mean 'after'. There is a danger in this straightforward formulation, however, which is that in the rush to announce a post-modernism or a post-modernity, the complexity of the modern is effaced to create a caricature of the thought, literature and politics of the past. If this happens, then the postmodern itself becomes little more than a trite discourse whose only interest is its fashionable focus on a vision of the contemporary that is entirely cut off from everything that might have led up to it, or indeed might persist within it. Also, if the modern is the age of the new, of development and innovation as the grand narratives progress and capitalism extends its net to capture hitherto isolated cultures, then it is difficult to see these versions of the postmodern as anything other than the latest developments of modernity rather than something qualitatively different. In the light of this, an important question for anyone wanting to understand the postmodern must be, 'what can the "post-" actually signify?'

In a short but very important essay called 'Note on the Meaning of "Post-"', written in 1985, Lyotard attempts to tackle precisely this question by suggesting that its relation to the modern takes the form of a tripartite structure. Identifying three versions of the relationship between the modern and the postmodern, he explores the problems that each one faces and the opportunities they offer. By outlining each in turn, and showing how it relates to the others, this essay builds up a clear and detailed picture of the situation of contemporary culture, its relations with other preceding cultures, and the challenges that face the postmodern critic.

The first version of the postmodern that Lyotard identifies develops from the sorts of arguments found in the work of Toynbee and the architectural theorists such as Jencks and Frampton which present it as a transformation from one period or style to the next. For Lyotard,

> this perspective is that the 'post-' of postmodernism has the sense of a simple succession, a diachronic sequence of periods in which each one is clearly identifiable. The 'post-' indicates something like a conversion: a new direction from the previous one.
>
> (1992: 76)

This account identifies the postmodern as a new period, style or fashion that supersedes earlier ones. Thus, for example, postmodern architecture with its critical regionalism and double-coded ironic citation replaces the universalism of the modernist International Style as uniformity falls from fashion. The problem, for Lyotard, with this account is that it presents the postmodern as little more than the next stage of historical development: another step in the progress of the grand narratives of modernity. If, however, these grand narratives can no longer function to guarantee progress, how can this account engage fully with the range of problems and challenges that we face today?

This question leads to a second version, which appears as a direct reaction to the implications of the first, and identifies the postmodern as a moment at which innovation and development can no longer be equated with progress. Postmodernism thus marks,

> a kind of decline in the confidence that, for two centuries, the West invested in the principle of a general progress of humanity. . . . It is no longer possible to call development progress. It seems to proceed of its own accord, with a force, an autonomous motoricity that is independent of us. It does not answer to demands issuing from human needs. On the contrary, human entities – whether social or individual – always seem destabilised by the results and implications of development.
>
> (1992: 77–8)

This version, which is similar in principle to what was presented in *The Postmodern Condition*, identifies the postmodern as a loss of faith in progress and a splintering of the universal projects of speculation and emancipation into a vast field of competing projects and narratives. The difficulty here, of course, is what space this leaves for critique and transformation, as, without rules or the possibility of consensus, what grounds are there (apart from mere anarchist delight in disruption) to challenge the values of the culture we inhabit? If we have lost touch with reason and reality entirely, what is the point of substituting one set of arbitrary theories and practices with another?

The third version of the postmodern is based on the apparently a-historical stylistic account of postmodernism that was introduced towards the end of Chapter 1. Lyotard describes it in the following manner:

> The question of postmodernity is also, or first of all, a question of expressions of thought: in art, literature, philosophy and politics. . . . [It involves] a kind of work, a long, obstinate, and highly responsible work concerned with investigating the assumptions implicit in modernity. . . . [It is] a working through (*durcharbeiten*) performed by modernity on its own meaning.
>
> (1992: 79–80)

Here, the postmodern does not simply replace the modern, but rather performs a continual rereading and critique of modern values and projects. Postmodernity is not a new age, but rather the name for a collection of critiques that seek to challenge the premises of those discourses that have shaped modern experience. It is thus a critical attitude within the modern rather than a replacement of it. The difficulty here, though, is that of failing to recognise the profundity of the transformations that are taking place in contemporary technology, communications and communal existence. If we are still part of the modern, which as we shall see has always been more than capable of performing its own self-critiques, why bother with the term 'postmodern' at all?

Each of the three versions of the postmodern is distinct from the others, each has had its supporters and detractors, and yet each also produces fundamental problems for the critic. For Lyotard, and this is what makes the essay so important, it is not simply a question of choosing one version of the postmodern from these three alternatives. Each one, taken individually, has serious flaws. Rather, all three must be put into play at once in any workable account of postmodernism or postmodernity. Of course things have changed (the first version): that there are new fashions, styles and technologies is incontrovertible. Of course the organisational structures of earlier times have ceased adequately to explain the world in which we live (the second version): traditional values, laws and alliances have fallen away and contemporary culture seems, as a result of this, to have become a site of incessant conflict and transformation. To deny this would be to shut one's eyes before the complexities of today's international politics. But, equally, of course these changes have emerged from the projects and tensions of the modern (the third version): to turn one's back on modernity as simply outmoded is to lose one's bearings on the present entirely, and the only way to grasp the present is in terms of its development from modern history and with the critical resources that the various discourses of modern thought have provided. What is required of the postmodern critic, then, is the ability to think in terms of all three versions at once without forgetting the conflicts and tensions between them.

This is no straightforward process. Quite how these three apparently very different versions of the postmodern might be made to work together is difficult to see. While not wholly opposed, each contains key themes that contradict the others. Understanding them as a tripartite structure will require a good deal of investigation and argument. This, though, will be the task of the rest of this book. In the process of this investigation, what will emerge is a picture of what is at stake in the post-modern, as well as an introduction to its impact across a wide range of cultural, social, political and philosophical areas. Most pressing of all, however, must be a more detailed understanding of what is meant by the term 'modernity'.

DEFINING MODERNITY

In order to understand the implications of the postmodern, it is vital to have some sense of what modernity might be. As Lyotard's arguments demonstrate, if postmodern theory is going to be able to produce any form of radical critique of contemporary culture and society, it must engage with the ideas, arguments and conflicts of the modern from which today's world emerges. To argue that modernity is simply finished or outmoded is, as this chapter and those which follow will attempt to show, actively to forget many of the tensions that form the basis of postmodernism and postmodernity, and, as a consequence, to fail to understand the insights that they generate. As Linda Hutcheon makes clear, the terms 'postmodernism' and 'postmodernity' actively 'incor-porate that which they aim to contest' by including and modifying the word 'modern' within themselves (Hutcheon, 1988: 3). In other words, the very construction of the terms themselves points to an important fact: the postmodern only makes sense as a modification of the modern that at once contains and contests its categories, ideas and problems. So how might we begin to understand modernity as the epoch of the progressive grand narrative in more detail? And what sort of postmodernity is capable of responding adequately to its dissolution?

Modernity, put simply, is the period of the new. As the American cultural critic Marshall Berman points out with a good deal of force in his important book *All that is Solid Melts into Air*, it marks a 'maelstrom of perpetual disintegration and renewal':

> To be modern is to find ourselves in an environment that promises us adventure, power, joy, growth, transformation of ourselves and the world – and, at the same time, that threatens to destroy everything we have, everything we know, everything we are . . . it pours us into a maelstrom of perpetual disintegration and renewal, of struggle and contradiction, of ambiguity and anguish. To be modern is to be part of a universe in which, as Marx said, 'all that is solid melts into air'.
>
> (Berman, 1982: 15)

If this notion of a modernity that is made up of struggle, disintegration and contradiction is taken seriously, then the idea of its simply being replaced by the postmodern becomes both untenable and trivial as such a postmodern would be little more than just another phase of modernity's constant self-transformation. In fact, much of the rhetoric of Berman's description of modernity will be familiar from some aspects of the discussions of the postmodern by Jameson, Hutcheon and Lyotard that have already been introduced. The central claim of Berman's argument, that to be modern is to be confronted with disruption and change as everything around one 'melts into air', bears striking resemblances to both Jameson's idea of schizophrenic depthlessness and Lyotard's analyses of the dehumanising effects of progress. The modern and the postmodern, it seems, share a number of key characteristics. How, then, can one identify the important differences between them?

What needs to be grasped is how the postmodern might function as something other than just one more in a series of changes in a continually self-renewing modernity. And, in order to do this, it is vital to develop an understanding of the political and philosophical discourses brought together under the title of the modern. What is necessary, then, if the postmodern is going to be thought of as a critical formation that is capable of reacting to contemporary society, thought and culture in a productive way, is an analysis of its relation to the modern that opens up the complexity and radical potentials of both discourses. To provide this, it is important to examine some of the theories that have shaped modern thought and politics, and to show the ways in which writers who are often identified as postmodern have adopted, challenged or transformed them.

As the passage from *All that is Solid Melts into Air* cited earlier argues, modernity is a discourse that takes change and transformation as its central premise. According to Berman, the period in which this process of change really gets under way begins at the end of the eighteenth century, and extends its influence across the range of human experience:

> The maelstrom of modern life has been fed from many sources: great discoveries in the physical sciences, changing our image of the universe and our place in it; the industrialisation of production, which transforms scientific knowledge into technology, creates new human environments and destroys old ones, speeds up the whole tempo of life, generates new forms of corporate power and class struggle; immense demographic upheavals, severing millions of people from their ancestral habitats, hurtling them halfway across the world into new lives; rapid and often cataclysmic urban growth; systems of mass communication, dynamic in their development, enveloping and binding together the most diverse people and societies; increasingly powerful national states, bureaucratically structured and operated, constantly striving to expand their powers; mass social movements of people, and peoples, challenging their economic and political rulers, striving to gain some control over their lives; finally, bearing and driving all these people and institutions along, an ever-expanding, drastically fluctuating capitalist world market.

(1982: 15)

According to Berman, then, modernity is a period of constant transformation that affects all aspects of experience from science and philosophy to urbanisation and state bureaucracy. Nothing in life is exempt from modern upheaval as the economic, political and philosophical discourses that govern social interaction are subject to continual revolutions, which in turn transform utterly the everyday lives of individuals and communities. Berman identifies changes in knowledge, power relations, the environment, communication, bureaucracy and the markets that perpetually dissolve any sense of stability or tradition that might bind people together. To be modern, he argues, is to be caught up in the inevitable progress of history: to have one's roots swept away into the past as one journeys into a future that promises to be radically different.

What Berman catches in his description of modernity is the sense of the rapid, inevitable and continual change that shapes human life. To be modern is to be constantly confronted by the new. If this is the case, it follows that, just as with the postmodern, the precise date for the origin of modernity will be difficult to specify: when does progress begin? Where does this transformation come from? Can one even imagine a time without change? Berman's analysis of the modern locates its beginnings in the Industrial Revolution that took root in European and North American culture at the end of the eighteenth century and throughout the course of the nineteenth century. There are, however, many other descriptions of the founding moments of the modern. Some identify the modern with other developments at the end of the eighteenth century such as American independence, which saw the birth of the contemporary world's great superpower, the French revolution with its invocations of equality and human rights, and the wars that consumed Europe for the next twenty years, as well as the revolutions in philosophy, science and the arts that accompanied these events (this approach is developed in texts such as Eagleton, 1990, Habermas, 1987 and Lyotard, 1984). Some critics locate the beginnings of modernity much earlier by exploring the development of Christian theology which finds a key interpreter in the figure of the theologian Saint Augustine who lived and worked during the fourth century (see Hegel, 1975 and Lyotard, 2000 for examples of this). Some relate it to the period of European expansion that began in the Middle Ages and developed into the colonial conquest and imperialism that drove nineteenth-century industrialisation (for example, Bhabha, 1994 and Said, 1985). For others, the key period of transition to the modern is the Renaissance, which began in Italy during the fifteenth century and quickly spread through Europe issuing in the birth of the modern subject in the philosophy of René Descartes, the realignment of the cosmos in Copernicus's discovery that the Earth moves around the Sun, and the invention of perspective in artistic representation (see, for examples, Heidegger, 1977 and Baudrillard, 1983a). Yet others identify modernity with artistic modernism and locate it towards the end of the nineteenth and beginning of the twentieth century, and argue that it reaches its apotheosis in the industrialised slaughter of the battlefields of the First World War (Jameson, 1990 and Thacker, 2003).

Whichever one of these alternatives is chosen, modernity comes to be identified as a period guided by humankind's striving for continual progress. This idea is captured in Lyotard's idea of the grand narratives, introduced earlier in this chapter, which draw all forms of knowledge together under the auspices of speculative development and the advance of emancipation. Jameson makes a similar case when he argues that 'Modernity is not a concept but rather a narrative category' (2002: 94). What he means by this is that there is no point in just choosing one of the periods outlined in the last paragraph as the true origin of modernity and conceptualising the modern according to a single governing criterion such as the era of capitalism, the epoch of perspective or the period of subjectivity. Rather, each of these categories functions as an aspect of the modern story that describes historical transformation across the range of disciplines, periods and locations.

For both Jameson and Lyotard, then, modernity is a narrative construct: the ways in which one links together the events, people and ideas of the past to produce an account of the meaning of the present determine the ways in which that present can be seen as an outcome of the past and a precursor to the sort of future that forms the basis of one's projects. Narratives of modernity can, for Lyotard and Jameson, be drawn from a range of religious, philosophical or political discourses, and each gives a different account of the modern. So, for example, a capitalist version of modernity might see the events of the Industrial Revolution as a sign of progress as society generates more wealth and people become freer to choose the sorts of lifestyle they desire (see, for example, Fukuyama, 1992), while a socialist account of the same events might produce a narrative that focuses much more on the growing divisions between the rich and the poor and the increasing exploitation of the workers who become little more than cattle driven into the factories to become the fodder for a future that is only of benefit to their bosses (see

texts such as Berman, 1982, Callinicos, 1989 or Lyotard, 1993). A sociological account of modernisation might focus on the changes of cultural
institutions and interactions between communities (see Lash, 1990)
while one based on the history of ideas might analyse the developments
in scientific knowledge, philosophy and human understanding solely in
terms of an abstract idea of the accumulation of knowledge (see Russell,
2000).

In the midst of this maelstrom of ideas, narratives and experiences, the
task facing modern criticism is to discern the rules, systems and values
that underpin development. In the words of one of the most important
thinkers of modernity, the late eighteenth-century German philosopher
Immanuel Kant,

> Since the philosopher cannot presuppose any individual purpose
> among men in their great drama, there is no other expedient for him
> except to try to see if he can discover a natural purpose in this idiotic
> course of things human. In keeping with this purpose, it might be
> possible to have a history with a definite natural plan for creatures who
> have no plan of their own.
>
> (Kant, 1963: 12)

In other words, the task Kant sets for the critic of modernity is to discern
beneath the apparent chaos of day-to-day existence a 'plan', what Lyotard
calls a 'grand narrative', that drives and determines the path of history and
charts a rational future in which people will be free to determine their
own destinies. The impulse behind the work of many of the key modern
thinkers has been to identify the driving forces that organise modernisation and progress, and to produce systems and theories that guide
human development towards more just and fair ends. If the world seems
to be caught up in a state of perpetual flux, contradiction and transformation, they set themselves the task of explaining how humanity has got
to where it is, criticising its errors and aberrations, and identifying ways
in which it can improve its lot in the future. Thinkers and critics who
follow this course partake in what the contemporary German philosopher
and social theorist Jürgen Habermas calls the 'discourse of modernity'
(Habermas, 1987).

JÜRGEN HABERMAS AND THE DISCOURSE
OF MODERNITY

Habermas's work is vital to any discussion of the modern and the post-modern as he produces one of the most sustained and persuasive analyses of the political, philosophical and ethical interventions of modern criticism in his attempt to defend modernity against its postmodern detractors. In the essay 'Modernity: An Unfinished Project', first given as a lecture in 1980 (and translated in Passerin d'Entrèves and Benhabib, 1996), and his book, *The Philosophical Discourse of Modernity* (1987), he develops a rigorous account of modern thought, politics and culture that remains extremely influential in debates about modernity and postmodernity today. Broadly speaking, he follows Berman's notion of modernity as a period of continual transformation, arguing that the 'concept of modernity expresses the conviction that the future has already begun: it is the epoch that lives for the future, that opens itself up to the novelty of the future' (1987: 5). He acknowledges, however, that modernity has multiple points of origin and many precursors in history. On the basis of this multiplicity, he argues that what needs to be studied is modernity's self-understanding – its 'philosophical discourse'. Habermas locates this specific 'discourse of modernity' as emerging at the beginning of the nineteenth century in the self-reflexive turns taken by philosophers, scientists and artists as they began to question the relationships of their disciplines with the revolutionary historical changes occurring at that time. Even if aspects of the modern emerged in earlier periods, Habermas argues, its self-understanding as a movement begins with the philosophical systems of Kant, G.W.F. Hegel and their contemporaries. In order to introduce this important account of modernity, it is useful to explore in some detail three key aspects of the discourse that Habermas's critique brings to the fore: the emancipation of subjectivity from mystical and religious world-views, the idea of history as the story of the rational progress of humanity, and the possibilities of resistance to the commodification of daily life. These three themes are as vital to postmodern critique as they are to modern discourse, and the next three chapters will examine each of them in much more detail. First, though, it will be useful to introduce the ways in which Habermas presents them.

In 'Modernity: An Unfinished Project', Habermas argues that modernity is characterised by a

> separation of substantive reason, formerly expressed in religious or metaphysical world-views, into three moments, now capable of being connected only formally with one another. . . . In so far as the world-views have disintegrated and their traditional problems have been separated off under the perspectives of truth, normative rightness and authenticity or beauty, and can now be treated as questions of knowledge, justice or taste respectively, there arises in the modern period a differentiation of the value sphere of science and knowledge, of morality and of art.
>
> (Habermas, 1996: 45)

What he is suggesting here is that one of the consequences of the development of the scientifically and logically meticulous accounts of human existence that began to develop during the Enlightenment was a loss of belief in the religious mythologies that had hitherto provided all-encompassing explanations of nature, morality and experience. These explanations were shaken by the new sciences, and the question of what it is to be human had to be re-examined in the light of new understandings of nature, morality and psychology. Subjectivity therefore became a key category for thought, and the different approaches to human experience that its investigation generated developed different disciplines that explored the world in terms of truth, justice and beauty, or, to give them their philosophical titles, epistemology, ethics and aesthetics. The different ways in which these three disciplines, which as Habermas says can be 'connected only formally', are brought together in the constitution of subjective experience give rise to different forms of political and social organisation, and serve to place the question of the subject at the centre of modern discourse. One of the most sustained critiques of the modern carried out by postmodernists focuses on this notion of the construction of the subject as, to use the postcolonial critic Edward Said's term, 'a concrete universal' (1975: 321) that is a ground in which to anchor truth, justice and beauty. The consequence of this, as Habermas quite correctly recognises, is that to understand much of what is at stake in the relations and conflicts between modern and postmodern thought one must explore the questions of what subjectivity is and how it develops and interacts with others and the world. This will be the task of Chapter 3.

A second consequence of the rejection of mythology as a foundation for knowledge is the emergence of an awareness of the fundamental role that history plays in the construction of human identity and culture. The idea that there are eternal truths and transcendent structures that organise reality was gradually replaced by analyses based on notions of historical development and progress towards enlightenment and justice. At the beginning of *The Philosophical Discourse of Modernity*, Habermas cites a key passage from the preface to the *Phenomenology of Spirit*, written by the influential German philosopher G.W.F. Hegel and first published in 1807, which powerfully evokes this idea of progress and transformation:

> our time is a birth and transition to a new period. The Spirit has broken with what was hitherto the world of its existence and imagination and is about to submerge all this in the past; it is at work giving itself a new form. . . . [F]rivolity as well as the boredom that open up in the establishment and the indeterminate apprehension of something unknown are harbingers of a forthcoming change. The gradual crumbling . . . is interrupted by the break of day, that like lightning, all at once reveals the edifice of the new world.
>
> (Habermas, 1987: 6; see also Hegel, 1977: 6–7 (translation modified))

The central idea here, that we stand constantly at the brink of a world-wide transformation, is a key figure in the work of almost all of the thinkers who have come to be associated with the discourse of modernity. Hegel, writing in the German town of Jena as Napoleon's French revolutionary army defeated the Germans just outside the gates, presents the *Phenomenology of Spirit* as ushering in a new method of reasoning for the new age: a philosophical discourse of modernity to mirror and explain the social and political transformations that were then occurring with great rapidity across the world. Habermas picks up on this sense of progress in Hegel's work and claims him as 'the first philosopher to develop a clear concept of modernity', and one whom we have to understand if we wish to 'be able to judge whether the claim of those who base their analyses on other premises [postmodernists, for example] is legitimate' (1987: 4). For Habermas, the key aspect of modernity that

Hegel's work develops is the idea that reality and rationality are historically determined, and that humankind is capable of transforming itself as it progresses towards freedom, truth and communal understanding. From Hegel onwards, the question of what history is and how the development of reason can be charted is crucial and must be taken into account if one wishes to understand the status of modern thought today and to grasp the challenges launched against it by postmodern critics who frequently claim that progress and in some cases even history itself are finished. This will be explored in detail in Chapter 4.

Running alongside these philosophical developments, Habermas also detects the emergence of a modern analysis of politics and society, and the development of an argument that thought cannot ultimately be differentiated from the material social conditions that surround it. Central to this political critique of modernity, he argues, is the work of the nineteenth-century political philosopher Karl Marx:

> It was no longer intellectual elites who experienced the release of the lifeworld from boundaries fixed by tradition; in the *Communist Manifesto* Marx could already appeal to everyday experience when he traced 'the uninterrupted disturbance of all social conditions, everlasting uncertainty and agitation' back to the 'revolution in the modes of production and exchange'. . . . Only what has, since the start of the nineteenth century, been called a *social movement* can liberate mankind . . .
>
> (Habermas, 1987: 60–1)

In Marx's work, Habermas finds another key aspect of modernity: the idea that, since human nature is not divinely given or eternally fixed but develops from a social context which is historically mutable, this nature can be changed. In other words, he argues that modernity is a social and a political discourse as well as a philosophical one. If changes in culture and society can change human experience, then there is a point in challenging existing structures in order to liberate those who are oppressed or marginalised, and this struggle is a practical social one rather than just an intellectual exercise. The development of reason that is analysed by Hegel, he argues, is complemented by the ideas of progress and emancipation in Marx's socio-political analyses that take as a key premise the notion that 'the spell cast by the past over the present has to be broken; only in the communist future will the present rule over the past' (Habermas, 1987: 61). There is a vital idea here: the discourse of modernity is not simply a theoretical analysis of the times, but also seeks to provide a practical means of intervening in the continually changing material world so as to emancipate people or groups from the difficulties to which they are exposed by development. Put simply, modern discourses are not just about understanding the world; they also seek to transform it. One of the most controversial aspects of postmodern critique is its apparent rejection of modern Marxism-inspired ideas about revolutionary change and the attempt to find other means to alter society. Chapter 5 will explore the vexed relations and the political debates and conflicts between modern and postmodern political theories.

Central to Habermas's depiction of modernity, then, are three categories: subjectivity, history, and political resistance. Modern understandings of each of these concepts have come in for criticism by postmodern thinkers, and, in order to begin to show what might be at stake in postmodern critique, the next three chapters will explore these categories of modern thought and practice in more detail and introduce some of the postmodern challenges to them. Identifying some of the key thinkers of these categories, they will examine the philosophies produced by them and demonstrate how each constructs a different aspect of the discourses of modernity and the postmodern.

3

SUBJECTIVITY

The subject, the 'I' that experiences and interacts with the world, is a central category of modern thought, and one that many postmodern thinkers have, for a range of reasons, wanted to question. Subjectivity has become a site of conflict between competing theories and practices, around which questions of ethics, politics and representation have continually circled since at least the Renaissance. However, in recent times, due in part to the critiques launched against 'Man' by feminism, post-colonialism and queer theory, it has come under ever increasing pressure. According to Fredric Jameson, one of the key themes in contemporary critical theory that is enthusiastically taken up by postmodernism is 'the "death" of the subject itself – the end of the bourgeois monad or ego or individual' (1991: 15). This often-cited assertion of Jameson's has been echoed and expanded upon by a wide range of postmodern critics to explore areas as diverse as philosophical ontology, political theories of globalisation, contemporary poetry and the impact of popular cultural forms such as the music channel MTV on gender identity and sexuality. If the subject really is dead, it is certainly proving difficult to bury, and therefore requires investigation as part of an introduction to the postmodern.

The Routledge Companion to Postmodernism, edited by Stuart Sim, expands upon Jameson's assertion and provides the following helpful definition of the place of the subject in modernity and the postmodern:

Postmodernism has rejected the concept of the individual, or 'subject', that has prevailed in Western thought for the last few centuries. For the latter tradition, the subject has been a privileged being right at the heart of cultural process. Humanism has taught us to regard the individual subject as a unified self, with a central 'core' of identity unique to each individual, motivated primarily by the power of reason. . . . Rights and privileges could be ascribed to that subject, whose development and self-realisation came to be regarded as a central objective (if not *the* central objective) of Western culture. . . . [For] postmodernists, the subject is a fragmented being who has no essential core of identity, and is to be regarded as a process in a continual state of dissolution rather than a fixed identity or self that endures unchanged over time.

(Sim, 2001: 366–7)

This short definition sets out in broad terms some of the main differences between modern and postmodern conceptions of the subject. It is, however, merely a sketch of the outline, and if one is to grasp what is at stake in these differences a much more detailed discussion will be necessary. What is a subject exactly? How is it 'central' to modern Western culture? How is it linked to rationality and rights? What about other cultures? And what does it mean for postmodernism to 'fragment' or 'dissolve' it?

In order to be able to respond adequately to these questions, it is important to understand the ways in which the idea of the subject has been developed and contested in Western thought. This is the aim of this chapter. It will begin by exploring a central premise of modern philosophies of the subject: that at the heart of identity there is a 'thinking I' that experiences, conceptualises and interacts with the world. It will then go on to investigate some of the ways in which this 'I' has been questioned, challenged and problematised by more recent modern and postmodern theorists.

THE MODERN SUBJECT: DESCARTES, KANT AND WORDSWORTH

In the flux of modernity, philosophy has frequently sought to identify a fixed and stable point, from which perspective change might begin to be understood. More often than not, this point has been located within the human subject itself as a key agent in the development of knowledge and understanding. It is the subject who experiences, partakes in and reflects upon change, and the subject's ability to retain a sense of identity in the face of the transformations produced by history is vital if there is to be any possibility of making sense of development and progress. For many contemporary commentators, one of the key bases of modernity is to be found in the philosophy of the seventeenth-century French thinker René Descartes (1596–1650), whose construction of a modern account of subjectivity finds proof of existence in our ability to think and to recognise and reflect upon the processes of thinking.

According to Jameson, 'with Descartes, we . . . witness the emergence of the subject, or in other words, of the Western subject, that is to say, the modern subject as such, the subject of modernity' (2002: 43). Prior to Descartes, the human subject tended to be conceived as the product of external forces and plans – usually those of a divine being – subjected to the tides of providence or fate. In his book *Meditations on the First Philosophy* (1641), Descartes undertakes a thought experiment in which he systematically doubts everything about which he might be mistaken in order to find what remains as a basis for certainty, and through this procedure develops an account of subjectivity that locates identity in the consciousness of the subject her- or himself. In other words, by ridding himself of inherited ideas and prejudices, Descartes aims to discover a new foundation for thought. At the outset he declares that, 'I shall apply myself seriously and freely to the general destruction of all my former opinions' (1968: 95). This is not simply a capricious game, but is rather a method by which a secure ground for human experience can be demonstrated that is centred in the human being rather than some external agency such as the mind of God. By a process that seeks 'to rid myself of all the opinions I had adopted up to then, and to begin afresh from the foundations' (1968: 95), Descartes breaks from the past and traditional world-views to establish a new understanding of the basis of thought and action.

Nothing seems to escape the radical thrust of Descartes' doubt: all of his former thoughts, beliefs and experiences are systematically rejected as capable of being errors, deceptions or illusions. Disallowing the truth even of his sensory experiences on the basis that each of the senses is potentially open to being deceived by illness, madness, dreams, or the tricks of some evil spirit, Descartes finally reaches a point of certainty in the midst of his doubt:

> I had persuaded myself that there was nothing at all in the world: no sky, no earth, no minds or bodies; was I not, therefore, also persuaded that I did not exist? No indeed; I existed without doubt, by the fact that I was persuaded, or indeed by the mere fact that I thought at all. . . . So that, after having thought carefully about it, and having scrupulously examined everything, one must then, in conclusion, take as assured the proposition: *I am, I exist*, is necessarily true, every time I express it or conceive of it in my mind.
>
> (1968: 103)

Stated in its more familiar terms, 'I think, therefore I am', Descartes' argument finds within human experience a principle that acts as the basis for a systematic knowledge of the world. Irrespective of how deluded or false one's ideas of the world might be, the fact that one is thinking at all serves to prove that one exists. Having deduced the 'I think', Descartes goes on as the *Meditations* progresses to develop an account of our knowledge of the world. In order to do this, however, the idea of a benign deity must be reintroduced: if the 'I think' guarantees existence it only does so at the price of doubting all experience, and in order for this experience to be revalidated the notion of a God who provides us with truth must be assumed. The *Meditations* concludes with the declaration that 'For as God is no deceiver, it follows necessarily that I am not deceived' (Descartes, 1968: 168), an assertion that reinscribes the very theological principle that the argument had set out to challenge.

The consequence of this approach to subjectivity is what some philosophers refer to as 'dogmatic rationalism': we can be certain of our thoughts and ideas, but how they fit with the 'reality' outside of us is continually open to doubt unless one retains an unquestioned notion such as divine providence that guarantees the truth of our experience. In other words, we can approach the world scientifically and in a rational manner only if we assume a principle (that the world really is as it appears to us because, for example, God wills it to be so) that we cannot rationally prove.

Almost 150 years later, at the end of the eighteenth century, Immanuel Kant returned to Descartes' ideas and set out to provide a new account of subjectivity that would overcome the problems thrown up in the earlier philosopher's arguments. His aim was to 'describe the shared structures of our subjective consciousness which are the "condition of possibility" of *objective knowledge* . . . without having recourse to a divinity who guarantees the order of the world' (Bowie, 2003: 2). In other words, the problem he explores is how we can be sure that the types of experience and knowledge we have as individuals can be assumed to be the same as others' experiences and thoughts, and therefore count as objective. In what he calls his 'Copernican revolution', Kant argues that, rather than assume that appearances match exactly the 'reality' that lies behind them, if we can deduce universal structures that guarantee we all produce these appearances in the same way, they can come to count as objective knowledge themselves: 'If intuition must conform to the constitution of the objects, I do not see how we could know anything of the latter *a priori*; but if the object (as object of the senses) must conform to the constitution of our faculty of intuition, I have no difficulty in conceiving such a possibility' (Kant, 1929: 22). The task for Kant, then, is to demonstrate that the 'faculty of intuition', how human beings experience the world of objects, is universal and rationally consistent, and thus capable of providing the basis for arguments about reality.

Kant undertakes this task in three books that have become crucial resources for both modern and postmodern thinkers: the *Critique of Pure Reason* (1781), the *Critique of Practical Reason* (1788), and the *Critique of Judgement* (1790). These books set out to identify the basis of thought by setting limits that differentiate philosophical or scientific thinking from mysticism, fantasy, delusion or dogma. In the three *Critiques* Kant splits human experience into three different spheres: knowledge, morality and taste. These correspond to three types of philosophical enquiry: epistemology (the theory of what it is to know), ethics (the rules about how one should act) and aesthetics (the experiences of pleasure and displeasure that accompany perception).

The *Critique of Pure Reason* asks how we can have objective knowledge of the world by undertaking an enquiry into the conditions that make it possible for such knowledge to be generated. Kant argues that all knowledge must be based on experience. In other words, knowledge arises from the relation between mental concepts and physical perceptions. For this reason, he argues that knowledge only occurs within what he calls the 'limits of experience', and that claims about what exceeds experience are untrustworthy. Kant thus distinguishes between concepts, which are based on experience, and ideas, which provide the conditions for concepts but do not have corresponding objects. Ideas, he argues, regulate the way our concepts work, but cannot themselves be presented. Thus, an idea would be something like 'causality' as it structures all of our experiences but appears to us only in terms of specific instances such as the concept that my kicking a ball will cause it to fly through the air.

In the *Critique of Practical Reason* Kant is concerned to explain ethics. He sets out to deduce the fundamental principle of morality, and distinguish ethical actions from those based on other motives such as instinct or desire for profit. He argues that we can call an action good or moral only if the motive behind it is just. The basis for his notion of the just motive is the 'categorical imperative': the idea that one should act only on a maxim that one would want to be applied universally. So, for example, committing murder as an act of revenge is necessarily unethical because if the maxim of revenge were universalised everybody would be likely to end up dead; or, as Gandhi famously put it, 'an eye for an eye will make the whole world blind'. In terms of the analysis developed in the *Critique of Pure Reason*, the categorical imperative is an idea rather than a concept: it is the condition of possibility for freedom and moral action but does not have a corresponding object.

Between the accounts of epistemology and ethics in the first two *Critiques*, Kant sets up a division that cannot be crossed. By arguing that knowledge is bound by the 'limits of experience' which cannot be exceeded without falling prey to illusions and errors, he makes room for a separate ethical realm in which human freedom rests upon a 'categorical imperative' that is not reducible to knowledge because it is not generated by experience: it is a formal law, an idea, that is 'applied' to experience. This effectively splits the subject in two, differentiating its capacity to know from its ability freely to choose to act according to the formal moral law.

Kant's aim in the *Critique of Judgement* is to bridge the gap between epistemology and ethics opened up by the first two *Critiques*. In the first part of the book he discusses aesthetics as a possible means of achieving this. He splits aesthetics into two modes: the beautiful and the sublime. The former explores the feeling of pleasure generated by a sense of harmony between the subject and the world when that subject encounters something beautiful. The latter, the sublime, invokes a more complex feeling of a mixture of pleasure and pain that is generated by the grandeur or might of an experience that seems at once to attract and terrify us. The sublime, rooted as it is in disharmony and disruption, has become a vital figure in postmodern theory, as the discussion of Lyotard's 'An Answer to the Question, What is the Postmodern?' in Chapter 1 set out to show. The second half of the *Critique of Judgement* investigates teleology: the question of whether the world can rationally be thought to be naturally fitted to human ends. According to the vast majority of critics, neither of these discussions manages to reconcile the differences between the first two *Critiques*, and this leaves the Kantian system, the subjectivity it generates and the modernity that follows from it open to continual conflict as what Jürgen Habermas refers to as the three 'value-spheres' of truth, justice and sensation collide with each other in every experience that one has.

The result of Kant's three investigations into what makes cognition possible is that Descartes' idea of the subject is desubstantialised: the immediate link between the 'I think' and the 'I am' is broken so that the former becomes not a proof of existence but a place-holder in the realm of experience. The fact that the 'I think' and the 'I am' in Descartes' deduction are identical to one another allows him to move from the 'I think', via the 'I am', to raise and answer the question 'who am I?' (the answer to which is 'a thinking being'). It is this movement, based on the 'immediately identical' nature of their unity, which Kant rejects. Kant argues that 'it must be possible for the "I think" to accompany all my representations' (1929: 152) in order for there to be any experience at all, but it will do so differently in experiences based on knowledge, ethics or aesthetics, and therefore its relation to the being of the 'I am' will always occur differently. From this basis, Kant argues that the 'I think' is necessary for the generation of experience and yet, crucially, is itself completely unknowable. He acknowledges this when he states categorically that the '*I think* . . . cannot itself be accompanied by any further representation' (1929: 153).

What this means is that Kant's philosophy disrupts the identity at the heart of the Cartesian subject by separating the 'I think' from the 'I am' and denying the possibility of logically generating a final answer to the question 'who am I?' from the relationship obtaining between the two. This means that the 'I am', the self-identity, that was the result of Descartes' deduction appears to have lost much of its foundational force in Kant's discussion. It is a representation of the self generated from the 'I think' but it is split off from, and tells one almost nothing about, the 'I' that is thinking. The result of this is that although the identity of the modern subject (the 'I think') remains intact, who that subject is becomes much more a function of the experiences generated by the environment in which it exists than some natural or divine eternal essence or soul.

This Kantian sense of subjective mutability can be seen at work in the creation of character in a great deal of modern literature. The cultural critic Catherine Belsey points out that,

> It is readily apparent that Romantic and post Romantic poetry, from Wordsworth through the Victorian period at least to Eliot and Yeats, takes subjectivity as its central theme. The developing self of the poet, his consciousness of himself as poet, the struggle against the constraints of an outer reality, constitute the preoccupation of *The Prelude*, *In Memoriam* or *Meditations in Time of Civil War*.
>
> (Belsey, 1980: 67–8)

One of the best examples to support Belsey's assertion can be found in the construction of the narrator in William Wordsworth's poem *The Prelude*, which he began in 1798 and continued to develop and revise until his death in 1850. The poem tells the story of the development of consciousness from childhood to the maturity in which the poet-narrator becomes capable of writing the poem. It traces the experiences, vicissitudes and challenges of life in the period of the American, French and Industrial revolutions: the transformation of the world from the rural context of a late eighteenth-century childhood in the Lake District to the threats and disorientations offered by industrial London and revolutionary France. The meditative tone of the poem is continually interrupted by shocks, surprises and adventures that challenge and in extreme cases threaten to shatter the narrator's self-identity as he reels away in horror from wounded soldiers, prostitutes, blind beggars and the barbarities of war and revolution.

There is, however, a power within the narrating subject, the 'I' of the poem, that holds it on course: the guiding thread through the narrative is provided by the subjective consciousness of the narrator who is able to grasp, comprehend and express these experiences by remembering and linking them together in ways that make sense of them and present the story as 'the Growth of a Poet's Mind' (Wordsworth, 1995: xxvi). In this way, the processes of memory are presented as central to the structure of *The Prelude*, and by extension to the notion of a modern subject that the poem produces. Any experience, Wordsworth seems to argue, no matter how immediately traumatic, can contribute to the subject's growth when remembered and reconceptualised as an aspect of the self.

This procedure of remembering, comprehending and linking experiences and events gives rise to the famous description of the 'spots of time' that form the foundations of the subjectivity of the narrative voice of the poem:

> There are in our existence spots of time
> Which with distinct pre-eminence retain
> A vivifying virtue, whence, depressed
> By false opinion and contentious thought,
> Or aught of heavier or more deadly weight
> In trivial occupations and the round
> Of ordinary intercourse, our minds
> Are nourished and invisibly repaired.
> (Wordsworth, 1995: 478)

The point here is that the subject is presented as a site of resistance to the challenges of the modern world: memory acts as a defence mechanism that 'nourishes' and 'repairs' minds damaged by the contentions of the present, and allows the sense of psychological continuity and consistency to emerge. Through memory, the modern subject is capable of constructing a personal narrative of identity, grasping the present and judging how to respond to the future. In essence, the modern subject is the product of its ability to recall and synthesise the events that make up its life: memory generates identity and allows each of us to become an individual and unique human being.

This link between the 'Copernican revolution' in philosophy, the focus on the self in poetry and the onset of modernity is not coincidental: in the flux of change and transformation that writers such as Marshall Berman identify with modern experience, a stable point is called for to act as a basis from which this change can be thought. Through the ability to synthesise the myriad events, experiences and encounters that make up a life, the modern subject is presented as an anchoring point in modernity's 'maelstrom of perpetual disintegration and renewal, of struggle and contradiction, of ambiguity and anguish' (Berman, 1982: 15). As such, it can become the bearer of responsibilities and rights, a member of society and a freely acting agent of change.

DISRUPTING SUBJECTIVITY: FREUD, FANON AND CIXOUS

This notion of the subject as a synthesising agency that acts as the basis of knowledge, ethics and aesthetic experience, and is capable of resolving the vicissitudes of progress by comprehending the numerous challenges that it offers, has been the focus of critique from a wide range of modern and postmodern perspectives. According to many of its critics, this idea of subjectivity 'appeals (positively) to the notion of a core of humanity or common essential feature in terms of which human beings can be defined and understood' (Soper, 1986: 11–12) in a way that hides the most crucial differences between them and gives a false sense of the power of the subject to determine its own conditions of existence. In contrast to this humanism, a number of critical perspectives focus instead on the ways in which the subject is constructed by the conditions of its existence that are produced by the culture it inhabits. This critique of humanism is led most powerfully by psychoanalytic theory: 'By claiming to articulate the singularly human while dissolving the classical "man" . . . psychoanalysis exemplifies the simultaneous exaltation and disintegration of the subject, the sublime catastrophe that threads its way through modernity' (Brewster *et al.*, 2000: 7). Although not aligned with the postmodern by many of its proponents, psychoanalytic theory produces fundamental challenges to modern humanism, rewriting the subject in a manner that recalls Lyotard's third notion of the postmodern introduced earlier (see Chapter 2, pp. 43–4).

In this section, I want briefly to introduce three important critics of this humanism, all of whom are influential for or influenced by psychoanalytic theory: the so-called 'father of psychoanalysis', Sigmund Freud, the Algerian political thinker and psychoanalyst, Frantz Fanon, and the French feminist theorist, Hélène Cixous. Each of these writers demonstrates ways in which the modern subject is rather less stable and self-sufficient than humanism might assume. In the discussions that follow, I want to explore just two aspects of their work: the way that each produces accounts of the unconscious and desire. The reason for choosing to examine these aspects of the thinkers' work is that the challenges they present to the modern subject set the scene in important ways for postmodernism's radical questioning of subjectivity, which will be the focus of the final section of this chapter.

Sigmund Freud (1856–1939) is the first thinker to introduce a rigorous and developed analysis of the notion of an unconscious faculty of the human mind that acts as a supplement to consciousness, disrupts its processes of organising experience and further decentres the founding moment of the 'I think'. In the words of one of Freud's most influential successors, the French psychoanalyst and theorist Jacques Lacan, Descartes' assertion of identity should be replaced with a significantly more complex formula: 'I think where I am not, therefore I am where I do not think. . . . I am not wherever I am the plaything of my thought; I think of what I am where I do not think to think' (Lacan, 1977a: 166). This formulation, or, rather, series of formulations, is deliberately self-contradictory: the Cartesian subject is displaced from the centre of experience as thought and being are rigorously separated. In order to see what is at stake in this reformulation of Descartes, it is helpful to look in more detail at psychoanalysis's discussions of subjectivity, the unconscious and desire.

Freud's writings introduce the idea that human consciousness, which Descartes and Kant identify with the 'I think', is supplemented by an unconscious reserve. This unconscious, although we cannot experience it directly, has a significant influence on the desires, motivations and interactions that shape the course of our everyday existence. It is not simply a 'second consciousness' that contains all that we are not thinking about at the time, but is of a completely different order: according to Freud, unconscious processes should be understood as 'having characteristics and peculiarities which seem alien to us, or even incredible, and which run directly counter to the attributes of consciousness with which we are familiar' (1984: 172). In other words, there is something in us that is alien to our conscious self-identity, irreducible to the 'I think', and yet influences and even at times determines our thoughts and actions. The unconscious, Freud argues, is necessary for human life: it acts as a repository for all of those thoughts and impulses that are too disturbing for conscious reflection and are thus repressed by the mind. It functions as a defence mechanism that stores those impressions, experiences and desires that the conscious parts of the mind are unable to deal with, and thus protects us from harm. Once repressed, however, they do not cease to have affects; rather, their attempts to find their way into consciousness are the basis of our dreams, desires and everyday slips of the tongue, as well as the psychological problems that many people face.

The unconscious is not only a store for repressed thoughts like a psychic deep-freeze. Rather, according to Freud, it is a constitutive part of every action undertaken by the subject:

> Unconsciousness is a regular and inevitable phase in the processes constituting our psychical activity; every psychical act begins as an unconscious one, and it may either remain so or go on developing into consciousness . . . as it meets with resistance or not.
>
> (1984: 55)

In other words, everything we think, wish or do contains 'an inevitable phase' of unconscious activity. This means that the subject produced by psychoanalysis can never be fully self-aware or complete because the rational principles behind its thoughts and actions are necessarily supplemented by unconscious drives and desires.

If rational thought is always invested with an unconscious charge, Freud argues that our interactions with others are equally supplemented by desires that are beyond conscious control. He splits human motivation between two forces: the pleasure principle that hungrily strives after gratification, and the reality principle that allows us to defer pleasure for rational ends. Human life is a continual struggle for balance between these principles as we strive rationally to organise our drives and desires. In Lacan's interpretation of Freud, the concept of desire makes explicit the effect that the unconscious has on the modern notion of the subject by focusing questions of identity not on the self-certainty of the 'I think' but on the constitution of the self through a desiring intersubjectivity. Lacan's definition of desire is deceptively simple – 'desire is the desire of the Other' (Lacan, 1977a: 264) – but should not be passed over lightly. The capitalisation of 'Other' here invokes a technical idea in Lacanian psychoanalysis: it identifies what Lacan calls the 'symbolic order', the realm of language and culture in which we all exist. This implies that desire is cultural. What we find desirable is generated by the norms and values of the culture in which we live, even if it can focus on what that culture presents as perverse or unhealthy. As well as this, the 'of' in the statement develops a double relation: desire desires the Other, but also desires to be the object of the Other's desire (the French '*de*' in '*désir de l'Autre*' means both 'for' and 'from' (see Easthope, 1999: 97)). In other words, desire for Lacan is both the desire to possess and also, and at the same time, the desire to be desired by the possessed in return, and therefore rests on a series of interactions with others and the Other that must be taken into account for any analysis of who or what the subject is.

Desire shapes our sense of who we are and drives our every interaction with the world but, according to Lacan, remains impossible to fulfil as a reciprocal recognition between self and other is impossible: 'there is', he says pithily, 'no sexual relation' (1982: 143). This does not mean that there is no sexual activity; rather, what Lacan is pointing to is the impossibility of the 'true love' that would be the result of reciprocal recognition between two people. Desire is of the Other, the whole cultural order, not the other, the individual loved one, and so any relation with an other, Lacan argues, can be formulated in the following terms: 'I love you, but because inexplicably I love in you something more than you . . . I mutilate you' (Lacan, 1977b: 263). If our desires are generated by our cultural context and strive for recognition by that context, the desired person or object that we pursue is produced as a fantasy conjured by the symbols and images of our culture rather than loved for what they are in and of themselves, and our relations with them are driven by a continual urge to transform them into the impossible fantasy image. Desire, in short, can never be satisfied, and continually pushes the subject on to new objects and 'others'.

The concepts of the unconscious and desire produce a profound challenge to the self-knowing, self-legislating subject of modernity. We are driven by forces over which we have no conscious control, our identity is shaped by the recognition we receive from others, and the possibility of ever fully knowing ourselves is forever denied. The subject produced by psychoanalysis is fundamentally riven: split between consciousness and the unconscious, and torn between rationality and desire. Some of the cultural and political implications of this splitting are developed in the work of Frantz Fanon and Hélène Cixous. Each, for different reasons, sets out to challenge the modern myth of the universal subject 'Man'.

For Fanon, writing in the 1950s during the Algerian struggle for independence from French colonial rule, these categories of psychoanalytic theory provide a means to think the ways in which the colonial subject's identity is constructed by the colonist. The contemporary postcolonial critic Homi Bhabha describes Fanon's disruption of the modern subject in the following manner:

> For Fanon such a myth of Man and Society is fundamentally undermined in the colonial situation where everyday life exhibits a 'constellation of delirium' that mediates the normal social relations of its subjects. . . . The representative figure of such a perversion, I want to suggest, is the image of post-Enlightenment man tethered to, *not* confronted by, his dark reflection, the shadow of colonised man, that splits his presence, distorts his outline, breaches his boundaries, repeats his actions at a distance, disturbs and divides the very time of his being. This ambivalent identification of the racist world . . . turns on the idea of Man as his alienated image, not Self and Other but the 'Otherness' of the Self inscribed in the perverse palimpsest of colonial identity.
>
> (Bhabha, 1986: xiv–xv)

This notion of the 'Otherness of the Self' has become the basis of one of the most trenchant forms of critique of humanism in contemporary critical theory. The colonial subject, caught in the oppressor's gaze, is split, distorted, breached and disturbed, unable to reconcile her or his self-image with the images that are projected back by others. Equally, although in different ways, the coloniser's identity is shaken by the relation with a colonised subject whose common humanity is at once denied and invoked by the politics of colonial discourse.

In an extremely influential essay from the book *Black Skin, White Masks*, which is entitled 'The Fact of Blackness' (1986: 109–40), Fanon explores the effects of racism on the construction of the subject and the production of identity. The essay is written in the style of an interior monologue that is punctuated by the voices of others who identify the narrator in racist terms: ' "Dirty nigger!" Or simply, "Look, a Negro!" ' (Fanon, 1986: 109). Each punctuation – whether it is racist abuse, the fear of a child in the street, poetry, music or the writings of an influential philosopher – strips away another layer of the narrator's self-identity:

> I came into the world imbued with the will to find a meaning in things, my spirit filled with the desire to attain to the source of the world, and then I found I was an object in the midst of other objects. Sealed into this crushing objecthood, I turned beseechingly to others. . . . I stumbled, and the movements, the attitudes, the glances of the other fixed me there, in the sense in which a chemical solution is fixed by a dye. I was indignant; I demanded an explanation. Nothing happened. I burst apart. Now the fragments have been put together again by another self.
>
> (Fanon, 1986: 109)

In the colonial situation the desire of the Other, manifested as either blatant or subtle racism, turns the subject into 'an object in the midst of other objects' and shatters identity. The will for meaning that drives Enlightenment thought is rejected by a racist culture and replaced by a continual rebuilding of the self as the narrator moves from person to person, text to text, misidentification to misidentification in the search for identity and subjecthood. Taking the psychoanalytic notion of subjectivity as mutable and produced through unconscious desiring interactions with others, Fanon's essay explores the implications of this racism for the construction and fragmentation of identity. The other, caught up in the cultural symbolism of the Other, sees not a humanist individual, but rather the 'legends, stories, history' attached to blackness: 'I was responsible at the same time for my body, for my race, for my ancestors . . . and I was battered down by tom-toms, cannibalism, intellectual deficiency, fetishism, racial defects, slave-ships' (Fanon, 1986: 112). As Wordsworth's *The Prelude* demonstrates, individuality is built from memories and associations, but when these are generated in a culture that denies one's humanity, the comprehension of the self as whole becomes impossible. Identity becomes a masquerade as one attempts to 'fit in': in this case, a series of 'white masks' to hide the 'black skin'.

According to both Fanon and Bhabha, this shattering of subjectivity does not apply only to the colonised, the coloniser's identity is equally troubled: quoting Fanon's statement that 'The Negro is not. Any more than the white man', Bhabha argues that the 'familiar alignment of colonial subjects – Black/White, Self/Other – is disturbed with one brief pause [the full stop after 'not'] and the traditional grounds of racial identity are dispersed, whenever they are found to rest in narcissistic myths of Negritude or White cultural supremacy' (Bhabha, 1986: ix). What Fanon's essay demonstrates is that the self-centred, self-certain universal subject is impossible: subjectivity is generated through the interactions with others that take place in the realm of culture, of the Other, and if that culture is itself as disjointed as it is in the colonial and postcolonial world then identity too will necessarily be fragmentary.

A related critique of modern subjectivity is developed in Hélène Cixous's essay 'Sorties: Out and Out: Attacks/Ways Out/Forays' (Cixous and Clément, 1986: 63–132). This essay explores the limitations of the modern subject by investigating the ways in which sexual difference generates identity positions. Sexual difference is not simply a physical difference that 'clothes' the a-sexual 'I think' in a physical body. Rather, because of its cultural history and production, it is much more problematic than the idea of a straightforward binary distinction between male and female would suggest. Cixous argues that the opposition between man and woman has accrued a whole range of cultural significations that generates a field of power relations that dispossess women of their voices, identities and the capacity to act. The essay begins with the question 'Where is she?', a list of oppositions such as 'Activity/Passivity', 'Head/Heart' and 'Man/Woman', and the argument that,

> Everywhere (where) ordering intervenes, where a law organises what is thinkable by oppositions (dual, irreconcilable; or sublatable, dialectical). And all these pairs of oppositions are *couples*. Does this mean something? Is the fact that Logocentrism subjects thought – all

concepts, codes and values – to a binary system, related to 'the' couple, man/woman?

(Cixous, 1986: 63–4)

For Cixous, all of the oppositions that make up Western culture are tied up with power relations, and all come to rest on '*the*' opposition between man and woman. Any opposition, she argues, organises the two terms it comprises in a hierarchy that presents one as active and the other passive, and 'Organisation by hierarchy makes all conceptual organisation subject to man. . . . Traditionally, the question of sexual difference is treated by coupling it with the opposition: activity/passivity' (1986: 64). In other words the categories and oppositions that make up a culture's values are premised on an organisation of thought in which descriptions of the feminine are determined by masculine categories of order, opposition and hierarchy. This has a crucial effect on the production of subjectivity.

In this sort of masculine culture, which for Cixous is the culture of Western societies, women's identity is bound up with the subordination of the feminine so that subject positions are mapped out in advance which prevent the assertion of female independence: boys are perceived to be active, aggressive, assertive, for example, whereas girls are generally seen as passive, sympathetic, nurturing. The response to this that Cixous espouses is not, however, an assertion that women can unproblematically adopt a masculine identity so as to compete on equal terms with men, but rather that the opposition itself should be resisted so that the multiplicity inherent in all identities can be explored. To this end, Cixous proposes embracing a bisexual notion of identity which, rather than accepting the masculine structures of organisation, revels in difference and dispersal:

Bisexuality – that is to say the location within oneself of the presence of both sexes, evident and insistent in different ways according to the individual, the nonexclusion of difference or of a sex, and starting with this 'permission' one gives oneself, the multiplication of desire's inscription on every part of the body and the other body. . . . To say that woman is somehow bisexual is an apparently paradoxical way of displacing and reviving the question of difference.

(1986: 85)

This notion of bisexuality is not simply a description of sexual practice, but rather calls for the recognition of the multiplicity of drives and desires within any subject and their irreducibility to a straightforward binary logic. One is not simply a woman or man, with all of the cultural coding that goes along with this. Instead, Cixous argues that a feminist criticism must explore the ways in which differences within the subject can be continually opened up to new forms of exploration and challenge. To this end she presents the idea of a feminine writing, an *écriture féminine*, that is able to affirm these differences, resist the closure of a male-orientated logic, and present subjectivity as a structure of continual renegotiations that transform the categories of patriarchy.

What Freud's, Fanon's and Cixous's critiques of the modern subject open up is the problem of positing an 'I think' as an origin of identity. If Kant's reworking of Descartes desubstantialises the 'I think', the challenges by these three psychoanalytic thinkers demonstrate the forces (the unconscious, desire, racism, sexism, etc.) that construct identity as a tenuous and fragmentary structure that is inherently social and therefore subject to the political conflicts of its cultural location. They thus set the scene for the destruction of 'the bourgeois monad or ego or individual' that Jameson identifies with the postmodern (1991: 15).

THE POSTMODERN SUBJECT: THE INHUMAN, CYBORGS AND MATRICES

The arguments of Freud, Fanon and Cixous stand at the threshold of the postmodern analysis of the subject. Each for its own reasons rejects the self-identity and self-certainty of the modern notion of Man as a universal human category arising from the 'I think'. This is not to say, however, that psychoanalysis, postcolonial criticism or feminism are all necessarily postmodern. Each discourse has proponents on either side of the modern/postmodern distinction, as well as those who refuse such an opposition. A more detailed discussion of the relations between these discourses and the postmodern will be undertaken in Chapter 5, which will look at the possibilities for political critique and action that the postmodern might offer in today's world. What I want to introduce here is the way in which the idea of identity as a performance and the impact of the technological innovations associated with postmodernity produce even more radical assaults on modern subjectivity.

A number of postmodern theorists and artists have explored the idea of identity as a performance that is infinitely mutable rather than being based on some essential nature. In the case of postmodern feminists, this notion of performative subjectivity is employed to disrupt the traditionally ascribed gender positions identified by Cixous. A key example can be found in the American artist Cindy Sherman's series of photographs *Untitled Film Stills* produced in the late 1970s and early 1980s, which depict her in a range of personas, from prostitute or career woman to wide-eyed innocent and film star, that run the gamut of clichés about female roles and refuse any sense of an essential selfhood. Equally, the novelist Angela Carter presents heroines such as Fevvers in *Nights at the Circus* (1984), the half-woman half-bird trapeze artist who is notoriously difficult for other characters to pin down, to challenge patriarchal ideas about feminine mystery and spectacle. Playful as these two examples undoubtedly are, they also have important political implications. As the postmodern feminist theorist Judith Butler explains, 'Just as the bodily surfaces are enacted as the natural, so these surfaces can become the site of a dissonant and denaturalised performance that reveals the performative status of the natural itself' (Butler, 1990: 146). This denaturalisation of the natural is taken even further by Jeanette Winterson in her novel *Written on the Body* published in 1992, in which the gender of the narrator is never revealed and the reader is constantly at a loss to know whether the protagonist is male or female, their relationships hetero- or homosexual, or if it really even makes a difference. Probably the most extreme example of this postmodern identity performance can be found in the work of the French performance artist Orlan, who in an ongoing project begun in the 1990s, which has been given such titles as 'The Reincarnation of Saint Orlan' and 'Image – New Images', is gradually transforming her appearance through surgery to create a composite of famous images of femininity that borrows from, among others, the forehead of da Vinci's *Mona Lisa* and the chin of Botticelli's *Venus*. The various operations have been filmed as theatrical events and the bloodstained costumes and instruments of the surgery are sold off as works in themselves. As well as scandalising public taste, this artistic experiment parodies the contemporary cultures of fashion and beauty, and raises questions about the discourses of femininity and, to say the least, the role of modern art.

If the identity of the modern subject has been challenged by performative critiques developed from psychoanalysis, feminism and post-colonialism, its central role in the generation of experience and knowledge is thoroughly undermined by contemporary theories and artistic representations of the relationship between the human and technology. Recent science fiction films such as Ridley Scott's *Blade Runner* and the Wachowski brothers' *The Matrix* have raised questions about the humanity of machines, and the potential for human beings to be reduced to components in a machine while being fed a simulation of 'real life', respectively. The cyberpunk literature of writers such as William Gibson, whose influential novel *Neuromancer* from 1984 explores the virtual reality of the world wide web, has generated similar questions about the relations between experience and identity. Technology, and its capacity to disrupt humanist ideas of the self-identical subject, has variously been presented as a threat and an opportunity: the postmodern philosophy of Lyotard has warned against the dehumanising effects of contemporary techno-science; and, on the other hand, the feminist theory of thinkers such as Donna Haraway has espoused the adoption of a cyborg identity as a positive means of challenging gender stereotypes.

The cultural productions that engage with the developments and challenges of science and technology frequently present pictures of a future in which human subjectivity and identity have become profoundly problematic. The centrality of memory that is so crucial for the Wordsworthian account of identity, for example, is questioned in a haunting scene from *Blade Runner* during which the female Replicant, Rachel, is informed of the fact that the memories that make up her identity are not her own but, rather, those of the daughter of her creator, Tyrell. Challenged in this manner, she is devastated as everything she assumed she was is torn away from her and she realises that she is not human. Equally, Neo's gradual awakening in *The Matrix* is presented as a stripping away of his sense of self (he even forgets to breathe having never actually done so in the 'real world' before) as he is rebuilt and, quite literally, programmed to become 'The One'. Each of these films presents a vision of the future in which the boundaries between reality and fantasy, the human and the machine, have become difficult to identify and must continually be renegotiated. For some contemporary theorists of the postmodern, though, this is not just science fiction but rather a possibility we face today.

Lyotard and Haraway present two different accounts of the politics of the impact of technological innovation on contemporary notions of subjectivity. The former, in his book *The Inhuman: Reflections on Time* (1991), argues that the subject produced by humanist thought is unable to withstand the encroachments of contemporary capitalism and technology, and is in danger of being eliminated, 'dehumanised', by them. This book develops the claim made in *The Postmodern Condition*, that today's capitalism acts as a 'vanguard machine' that drags 'humanity after it, dehumanising it' in the drive for ultimate efficiency (Lyotard, 1984: 63), and argues that the only resistance to this form of the inhuman is another inhuman that is at work in human subjectivity. In contrast to this technological inhuman, Lyotard claims that postmodern thought is able to identify an alternative form of the inhuman: the potential for being taken hold of by surprising and uncanny transformative possibilities that cannot be predicted, explained or mastered by technologically based systems of reason. He locates this sense of the inhuman in the 'anguish of a mind haunted by a familiar and unknown guest which is agitating it, sending it delirious but also making it think' (Lyotard, 1991: 2).

For Lyotard, then, the human is the product of a conflict between two inhumans: the inhuman systems of technology and capitalism that threaten to extinguish anything in the human that is not of value to them, and, within this same human, the uncanny strangeness of another inhuman that is a potential site of resistance. He argues that,

> the question I am raising here is simply this: what else remains as 'politics' except resistance to this inhuman [system]? And what else is left to resist with but the debt to which each soul has contracted with the miserable and admirable indetermination from which it was born and does not cease to be born? – which is to say, with the other inhuman? . . . It is the task of writing, thinking, literature, arts, to venture to bear witness to it.
>
> (Lyotard, 1991: 7)

Without the inhuman indetermination at its heart, the human ceases to be able to resist the first form of the inhuman, that of the developmental system. As Lyotard argues in a later essay, 'The right to this no-man's-land is the very foundation of human rights. . . . Humanity is only human if people have this "no-man's-land"' (Lyotard, 1997: 116). As the closing sentence in the long quotation above states, the task of post-modern writing, thinking, literature and art is to bear witness to this 'no-man's-land' and militate against the drive to exclude it from the systems that seek to explain entirely and control it. The means by which it can do this are generated by his analysis of the sublime that was introduced in Chapter 1, which presents 'the existence of something unpresentable' (Lyotard, 1992: 11) in every realism: in this case, a 'no-man's-land' at the heart of humanism. It is thus by rejecting the stable identity of the modern humanist subject that Lyotard's second sense of the inhuman stages a defence of humanity.

In contrast to Lyotard, who sees the rapid spread and development of technology as a threat, Donna Haraway urges postmodernists, and particularly feminists, to embrace it as a liberation from the sexism of modern culture. In her influential essay 'A Cyborg Manifesto: Science, Technology, and Socialist-Feminism in the Late Twentieth Century', from the book *Simians, Cyborgs, and Women: The Reinvention of Nature* (1991: 149–81), she argues that,

> By the late twentieth century, our time, a mythic time, we are all chimeras, theorised and fabricated hybrids of machine and organism: in short, we are cyborgs. The cyborg is our ontology; it gives us our politics. The cyborg is a condensed image of both imagination and material reality, the two joined centres structuring any possibility of historical transformation.
>
> (Haraway, 1991: 150)

For Haraway, the distinction between human and machine no longer makes sense: we have all become cyborgs, which she argues is 'a creature of social reality as well as a creature of fiction' (1991: 149). The figure of the cyborg is at once a result of the rapidly increasing developments of medical technology, which provide us not just with replacement prostheses such as artificial legs or hearing aids but also with mechanical devices to replace key organs such as the heart, and also an outcome of the imaginations of contemporary culture that is infested with robots, computers, thinking machines and other devices that have become humanised. One only needs to recall Arnold Schwarzenegger's *Terminator* films to notice the gradual humanisation of the android as it moves from being hunter to protector and saviour (and eventually, some might say, to governor of California). For Haraway, a recognition of the breakdown of a firm opposition between the human and the machine offers the potential for a transformative politics.

According to Haraway, the idea of the cyborg provides a means by which the oppressive binaries of sexual difference identified by Cixous can be reworked to produce multiple open structures of difference, thereby escaping the power relations of patriarchy:

> Cyborg imagery can suggest a way out of the maze of dualisms in which we have explained our bodies and our tools to ourselves. This is a dream not of a common language, but of a powerful heteroglossia. It is an imagination of a feminist speaking in tongues to strike fear into the circuits of the super-savers of the new right. It means both building and destroying machines, identities, categories, relationships, space stories.
>
> (Haraway, 1991: 181)

What the cyborg offers, then, is a means of challenging those dualisms that shape modern accounts of identity (self/other, subject/object, mind/body, etc.) by replacing them not with a 'common language' that codifies everything in the same way, as Lyotard's first form of the inhuman would do, but which introduces heteroglossia, the possibility of a multiplicity of tongues and idioms, into the language that we have. The result of this for the subject, Haraway argues, is that it becomes thinkable as a site of multiple identities, boundaries and desires: 'The cyborg is a kind of disassembled and reassembled, postmodern collective and personal self' (1991: 163). And this, she claims, 'is the self that feminists must code' (1991: 163).

While for Lyotard, then, the technologisation of contemporary culture threatens to dehumanise us and reduce us to cogs in the machine of capitalism, for Haraway this technology is something to be embraced because of the paths it opens up to transform the sexual hierarchies and stereotypes of modern culture. Each produces a challenging critique of the humanist individual, and develops an account of the postmodern subject that is radically fractured. It is important to recognise, though, that none of the cases discussed in this section simply dismiss subjectivity in its entirety. Both the idea of a fixed and immutable modern subject and the idea of a subject-free postmodernism are overly reductive. It is more accurate to acknowledge that that relationship between the modern and the postmodern is based on a continual renegotiation and disruption of subjective identity, a process that Lyotard recognises 'has been at work, for a long time now, in modernity itself' (1991: 34).

The gradual disruption of the idea of a self-conscious, self-sufficient subject that this chapter has charted also displays an increasing sense that identity is produced by the social, cultural and technological context from which it emerges. It therefore becomes a historically mutable structure that remains open to redefinition and transformation in the future. In order to explore what is at stake in this process of mutation, it is helpful to turn now to the question of history.

4

HISTORY

The second key aspect of modernity that Habermas's discussion in Chapter 2 focused on is the notion of historical development and progress towards more rational and just forms of social organisation and cultural interaction. This is one of the guiding ideas of modern thought, and is one that has been a key category for postmodern critics to question. Ideas of history have already been touched upon in other arguments explored so far. Chapter 2 also introduced Berman's analysis of the modern as a resolutely developmental world-view in which progress transforms every aspect of experience as new social and economic organisations generate new forms of identity and community at a rapidly increasing pace. We have also seen some of the postmodern responses to this idea of historical progress. Chapter 1 introduced Jameson's idea of postmodern depthlessness and the weakening of a sense of history, in which any idea of continuity with and development from the past has evaporated, and Hutcheon's notion of historiographic metafiction by which literary texts set out to challenge the received meanings of past events. Chapter 2 discussed Lyotard's arguments about the destruction of the modern grand narratives that identify and shape historical progress. Each of these questions the idea of development and progress that underlies the modern sense of historical change. Key questions that were left unanswered in all of these modern and postmodern arguments, however, include the following: what is at stake in this focus on historical progress? Why is history so important for both modern and postmodern thought? What sorts of history do they present? And how do these notions of history relate to the everyday experience of individuals and the cultures and societies they inhabit?

The claim made by critics such as Berman, Lyotard, Hutcheon, Jameson and Habermas is that with the advent of modernity history takes on a whole new meaning and value. This is not, of course, to argue that no histories were written before the onset of modernity. History has been an object of study from the very earliest societies, and chronicles noting the key events of their various cultures, from wars to the yields of harvests, were kept even in ancient times. The Greek writer Herodotus (*c.* 484–425 BCE) has often been referred to as the 'father of history', and his works chart the conflicts and adventures of Greek society during their encounters with the various cultures that surrounded them. He provides a catalogue of incidents, characters and interactions that covers a period of many years, and yet what he produces is very different from the historical thinking that underpins modernity. The philosopher Aristotle (384–322 BCE) characterises the ancient Greek notion of history by differentiating it from poetry in the following manner in the *Poetics*:

> The difference between the historian and the poet is not that one writes in prose and the other in verse. . . . The difference is that one tells of what has happened, and the other of things that might happen. For this reason poetry is something more philosophical and more worthy of serious attention than history; for while poetry is concerned with universal truths, history treats of particular facts.
>
> (Aristotle, 1965: 43)

The difference here is that while the poet deals with the possibilities of what might happen and is concerned with 'universal truths' of human nature, the historian's task seems to be little more than to chart particular 'facts' and events without drawing more general conclusions about their meanings or connections. The historian is, on this account, a mere chronicler who records what has happened without passing judgement.

This idea of history as dealing only with the particularity of individual events and therefore having a different focus from poetry or philosophy can still be seen to have currency in Renaissance England, particularly in the work of Sir Philip Sidney (1554–1586) who argues in his *Apology for Poetry* that,

> the historian, wanting the precept, is so tied, not to what should be but to what is, to the particular truth of things and not to the general reason of things, that his example draweth no necessary consequence, and therefore a less fruitful doctrine.
>
> (Sidney, 2002: 90)

Unlike the moral philosopher whose focus on universal precepts excludes particularity, or the poet who is capable of moving between the two extremes, the historian, according to Sidney, remains tied to individual events and is incapable of drawing consequences from them or using them to predict the future.

In contrast to Sidney or the ancient Greeks, modern accounts of history seek to combine the tasks that Aristotle allots to the poet and the historian, or that Sidney allots to those two and the philosopher, in order to record the particular things that have happened while, at the same time, demonstrating their necessity, universality, and their relations to one another and to the whole future progress of humanity. Modern history's aim is to present what French philosopher Jean-Luc Nancy, following Lyotard, refers to as 'the narrative of some grand, collective destiny of mankind . . . a narrative that was grand because it was great, and that was great because its ultimate destination was considered good' (Nancy, 1993: 144). Each event, important in itself of course, is fitted into a larger narrative and its lessons and implications are teased out to present it as part of the ongoing progress of humankind in which everyone has a stake.

The model for many of these modern historical grand narratives is the Christian Bible, which tells the story of the whole history of the world from the creation of Eden to the Armageddon of the last days and the establishment of the Kingdom of Heaven on Earth. All of the events and stories that are depicted in Christian mythology are linked together as aspects of an overarching story of salvation, and each individual is placed in the position where he or she can see what part they have to play in the story and how they relate to the world around them. Not only does it provide a historical chronicle, it also establishes a moral outlook that tells us how we should act and explains how and why the world appears to us as it does. It thus provides a structure in which all other narratives and events can be included, and through which they can be interpreted and explained as aspects of the providential scheme of God that will lead inevitably to human salvation. As the contemporary American writer Francis Fukuyama argues, 'The first truly Universal Histories in the Western tradition were Christian . . . it was Christianity that first introduced the concept of the equality of all men in the sight of God, and thereby conceived of a shared destiny for all the peoples of the world' (Fukuyama, 1992: 56).

Like the notion of subjectivity discussed in the last chapter, however, modern history also undergoes a process of secularisation. The mythical structure of the stories contained in the Bible is mirrored, supplemented and even refuted by a series of non-religiously-based grand narratives of progress and modernisation that seek to produce an understanding of the course of the world and the place of its inhabitants. Although their aims and projected outcomes may differ quite significantly, each of these tends to follow the same sort of narrative development and presents a similar type of all-inclusive system that shapes identity, experience and destiny. In order to introduce this process of thinking history as a secular progress towards the resolution of conflict and oppression, I want to examine the work of one of its most important and rigorous modern proponents, the German philosopher G.W.F. Hegel, and read his philosophical work alongside that of the most influential writer of the modern historical novel, his contemporary, the nineteenth-century Scottish author Walter Scott.

MODERN HISTORY: HEGEL AND SCOTT

The most influential thinker of the modern grand narrative is Hegel (1770–1831). There is not a single argument in his work that is not concerned with becoming, growth and progress, and the ways in which the world's continual transformation can rationally be comprehended. He produces an account of history, reason and society that generates a grand narrative which, in terms of Lyotard's two types that were introduced in Chapter 2, is both speculative and emancipatory. His writing strives to chart the progress of what he calls 'spirit' (*Geist*) as it moves inevitably towards a resolution of the conflicts and crises that face humanity and leads to a new world that is both self-comprehending and free. The term 'spirit' is central to Hegel's philosophy, and it has a wide range of meanings. Basically, however, spirit might be understood to point to the way a particular culture or period sees the relations between subjects and the world, the structures of their knowledge and morality, and the political organisations that govern their action. As the contemporary term '*Zeitgeist*' ('spirit of the times') suggests, it indicates the structures of belief and action for a particular age. History, according to Hegel, is made up of the succession of spirits that replace one another as the contradictions thrown up by earlier ones are reconciled and more powerful methods of understanding, interacting and governing are developed. In other words, each spirit presents a very different world-view as it identifies the core beliefs and principles of the society that generates it. For Hegel, history is not just a change from one spirit to another, but marks an inevitable and necessary progress from the less to more sophisticated and rational understandings of humanity and the world. So, for example, if the spirit of feudalism identifies as one of its aspects a very strict sense of a fixed hierarchy of social relations between the nobles and the ordinary population, the materialisation of a capitalist economy towards the end of this period throws up a contradiction within the social structure between the lords and a newly emergent and powerful business class that can only be resolved by a transformation of the whole social order and the adoption of a new world-view that is better attuned to the needs of the new economy. The aim of Hegel's systematic analysis of history is to explain and demonstrate the inevitability of this movement. The process that drives and charts this development of spirits through the reconciliation of conflicts and contradictions he calls 'speculative dialectics'.

Hegel's speculative dialectic describes a process of perpetual overturning of the relations between ideas and material reality that he identifies in every human endeavour. Each movement in it involves three steps: (1) a concept or state of affairs is taken as fixed and clear, but (2) on closer analysis contradictions emerge in it which, when worked through, result (3) in a more rigorously formulated concept or state of affairs that includes both the original and its contradictions within itself. This means that knowledge is constantly progressing through the stages of the dialectic as it comes closer and closer to a non-contradictory account of reality. The goal of knowledge is what Hegel calls the 'Absolute', by which he means both the organised totality of the different forms of knowledge and the freedom that results from the rational organisation of society. With the Absolute, Hegel argues, all contradictions and oppositions between ideas and realities are reconciled in a system of philosophical knowledge.

This speculative dialectic is crucial for all aspects of Hegel's philosophy. Accordingly, dialectic is not simply a feature of conceptual thought but also structures the development of things and processes in the world. In his book about ethics, politics and the state, the *Philosophy of Right* which was first published in 1821, Hegel claims that the idea from which 'philosophy starts in its study of the universe of mind as well as the universe of nature' is summed up in the formula that '*What is rational is actual and what is actual is rational*', and argues that because 'rationality . . . enters upon external existence simultaneously with its actualisation' (Hegel, 1952: 10) the world must always already be subject to the laws of reason, and therefore capable of being understood dialectically. This idea that the world is essentially rational and that reason is necessarily tied to reality enables Hegel to link together all of the different aspects of nature, technology, morality, politics and culture in a single overarching philosophical system that is capable of comprehending the relations between all of the different realms of experience according to the idea that they stand in dialectical relation to each other.

This equation of rationality and reality is central to Hegel's construction of historical progress as a dialectical movement and also to his idea that the movement of this dialectic is itself intrinsically historical. In his posthumously published *The Philosophy of History*, he states quite explicitly that 'reason governs the world, and . . . world history is therefore a rational process' (Hegel, 1975: 21). At the end of the *Phenomenology of Spirit*, he justifies this assertion by equating history with the development of spirit:

> [Spirit's] Becoming, *History*, is a conscious, self-*mediating* process. . . . This Becoming presents a slow-motion succession of Spirits, a gallery of images, each of which, endowed with all the riches of Spirit, moves thus slowly just because the Self has to penetrate and digest this entire

> wealth of its substance. . . . The realm of Spirits which is formed in this way in the outer world constitutes a succession in Time in which one Spirit relieved another of its charge and each took over the empire of the world from its predecessor. Their goal is the revelation of the depth of Spirit, and this is the Absolute . . .
>
> (Hegel, 1977: 492)

History is thus depicted as a series of dialectical movements in each of which the 'Self has to penetrate and digest [the] entire wealth of its substance'. Each new spirit is a new world-view: a new way of relating to reality, a new series of questions and problems, a new outlook or approach in the movement towards the Absolute that contains within it all that remains pertinent from the preceding spirits. History is thus brought under the auspices of reason as the succession of increasingly advanced spirits supersede each other to generate a movement towards 'their goal' which is 'the Absolute': the reconciliation of conflict and contradiction in a state that is free and just.

History thereby becomes the story of an inevitable progress as all of the individual desires, interests, events, changes and conflicts that make up a particular age are brought under the auspices of the progress of spirit by what Hegel calls the 'cunning of reason':

> The particular interests of passion cannot therefore be separated from the realisation of the universal; for the universal arises out of the particular and determinate and its negation. . . . Particular interests contend with one another, and some are destroyed in the process. But it is from this very conflict and destruction of particular things that the universal emerges. . . . It is what we may call the *cunning of reason* that it sets the passions to work in its service, so that the agents by which it gives itself existence must pay the penalty and suffer the loss.
>
> (Hegel, 1975: 89)

Because historical progress is itself encompassed by the speculative dialectic, the passions, desires, thoughts and actions of every subject are what make up this developmental movement. History is not an idea imposed from above on events, but emerges from the connections made between them by the 'cunning of reason'. What this means is that this 'cunning' must, according to Hegel, be at work behind the subject's every action, making that action, however arbitrary or negative it might appear, a meaningful stage in the movement towards the final Absolute: freedom. This should not, of course, imply that history is a seamless progress. Rather, it is a process of perpetual strife and conflict: a 'slaughter bench' or even an '*altar* on which individuals and entire nations are immolated' (1975: 212), as he memorably puts it. According to Hegel, however, even the most terrible and vicious injustices, wars and atrocities will lead in the end, through the resolution of the conflicts that give rise to them, to a better world and a more rational understanding of humanity and its interactions.

In Hegel, then, rationality guides the whole structure and development of human knowledge and experience as reason, reality and truth are transformed from the a-temporal universal structures that were the stuff of earlier philosophy into historical categories that are continually opened to change as ideas and institutions come into conflict. As the critic Paul Hamilton argues in his book *Historicism*, in Hegel philosophy itself

> becomes a history of these contradictory encounters, a dynamic chronicle revised at each stage by the transformation of what it is about. The history of the mind's constructions of reality is . . . as much a history of discontinuity – since both terms, mind and nature, repeatedly change their meanings – as it is one of continuity.
>
> (Hamilton, 1996: 47–8)

It is in this way that what Berman describes as the 'maelstrom of perpetual disintegration and renewal' (1982: 15) in its necessity and inevitability comes to be comprehended by modern thought as a grand narrative of progress.

An almost exact contemporary of Hegel's, the novelist Walter Scott (1771–1832), captures this idea of history as a development and transformation of the world that shapes human understanding and existence in his literary works. According to the influential Marxist critic Georg Lukács, Scott is the first and most important writer of the historical novel. It is not just that his novels were often set in the past that makes him this. Rather, what Lukács finds in Scott is a modern sense of the ways in which historical development produces the totality of relations that shape human identity and culture:

> Scott portrays the great transformations of history as transformations of popular life. He always starts by showing how important historical changes affect everyday life, the effect of material and psychological changes upon people who react immediately and violently to them, without understanding their causes. Only by working from this basis does he portray the complicated ideological, political and moral movements to which such changes inevitably give rise.
>
> (Lukács, 1969: 52)

Scott's novels, particularly those such as *Waverley, The Tale of Old Mortality* and *Rob Roy* that deal with the uprisings of the Scottish clans, present the whole range of classes, groups and identities that form a particular culture and period, and explore their interactions at moments of crisis or revolution. In *Waverley; or, 'Tis Sixty Years Since* published in 1814, for example, the fictional English hero Edward Waverley is caught up in the 1745–6 Jacobite rebellion in which the Scots under the leadership of Charles Edward, the young Stewart prince, attempted to overthrow the English monarchy and reclaim the throne for the line of James II (of England) and VII (of Scotland). Waverley meets with a range of people from lords to peasants, interacts with actual historical figures from the period, and takes part in historical events. Although fictional, the novel portrays real events and conflicts, and demonstrates the ways in which those events set the scene for Scott's contemporary culture (some sixty years on, as the subtitle of the novel indicates). This linking of the events of the story to contemporary culture sets up a sense of historical continuity that is entirely modern in its orientation. This sense is, as Lukács suggests, thoroughly Hegelian:

> if Scott's main tendency in all his novels . . . is to represent and defend progress, then this progress is for him always a process full of con- tradictions, the driving force and material basis of which is the living contradiction between conflicting historical forces, the antagonisms of classes and nations.
>
> (Lukács, 1969: 57)

As a result of Scott's innovatory narrative technique and as a consequence of his vast influence on nineteenth-century writing, this type of historical novel has became one of the key genres of modern literature as it is written and consumed in Europe and North America. As a literary form, it presents a view of history that is essentially modern, developmental and progressive, thereby resolving the splits between poetry, history and philosophy described by Aristotle and Sidney, and depicting progress as an inevitable universal movement.

POSTMODERNITY AND THE 'END OF HISTORY': FUKUYAMA AND BAUDRILLARD

For postmodern theory, the modern idea of progress has been challenged from a wide range of different perspectives, each with a different cultural and political orientation. This section will introduce the most radical of these challenges: the argument that contemporary culture has reached the 'end of history'. As the idea of history as progress implies, if there is a goal to development there must necessarily be the possibility that this goal will one day be reached and history will come to an end. This may come about through supernatural or temporal ends such as the biblical account of revelation or Hegel's idea of the emergence of freedom in the just society. The question that this gives rise to is whether this end has been reached by contemporary society (as Hegel sometimes seems to suggest of his own period) or, instead, whether our time marks the realisation that such an end (and by implication the whole notion of a progress towards it) has been shown to be impossible.

It is important to note first, however, that the idea of an 'end of history' does not imply that nothing more will ever happen. Rather, what the postmodern sense of an end of history tends to signify is, in the words of contemporary historian Keith Jenkins, the idea that 'the peculiar ways in which the past was historicized (was conceptualized in modernist, linear and essentially metanarrative forms) has now come to an end of its productive life; the all-encompassing "experiment of modernity" . . . is passing away into our postmodern condition' (Jenkins, 2001: 57). In other words, what has ended is not the production of events themselves, but rather our need or ability to form a narrative from them that demonstrates their coherent, developmental logic and points to a utopian future in which the conflicts and contradictions between them will have been resolved.

In this section I want to look at two versions of this so-called 'end of history' argument. The first, from the neo-conservative American critic Francis Fukuyama, sees modern history as having achieved its goal of universal freedom in the market-orientated liberal democracy of the United States. For Fukuyama, history comes to an end with the achievement of the modern aspirations towards freedom and justice, rather than in the more recognisable postmodern form of fragmentation and disruption. The second version, that of the French postmodern theorist Jean Baudrillard, presents the end of history as an abject failure of the modern aspiration to reconcile reason and the world. He argues that history has 'gone into reverse' (1994: 10) as the critical distance between rationality and reality that is necessary for us to understand or change the way things are vanishes in contemporary hyperreality. Each of these writers responds in his own way to Hegel's philosophy, contesting some aspects and recycling others.

Fukuyama's argument in *The End of History and the Last Man* (1992) that we are reaching the end of history by fulfilling the ideal of universal freedom has drawn a huge amount of both positive and negative critical commentary. Taking Hegel's dialectical approach to history as the movement towards the realisation of universal freedom as a point of departure, the book presents the case that 'While some present-day countries might fail to achieve stable liberal democracy, and others might lapse back into other, more primitive forms of rule like theocracy or military dictatorship, the *ideal* of liberal democracy could not be improved upon' (1992: xi). If this is the case, Fukuyama argues, then the realisation of liberal democracy in the West, and what he sees as its gradual spread to all other parts of the world, presents the idea that history 'as a single, coherent, evolutionary process' (1992: xii) is rapidly coming to an end. It is not that there will be no more events, inventions, innovations or changes, but rather that these will serve to support rather than undermine liberal democracy as an 'ideal' world order. According to this argument, we could see George W. Bush's 'war on terrorism' with its apparent attempt to spread American free-market liberal-democratic values throughout the Middle East and the developing world as a final step in the realisation of freedom. In fact, as Fukuyama claims in a discussion of the first Gulf

War: 'A large part of the world will be populated by Iraqs and Ruritanias, and will continue to be subject to bloody struggles and revolutions. But with the exception of the Gulf, few regions will have an impact . . . on the growing part of the world that is democratic and capitalist' (1991: 19). In other words, history has ended for those who matter: 'we' are liberal, 'we' are democratic, and if 'they' turn their backs on this it is not 'our' problem.

Fukuyama's case that the West is reaching the end of history rests on arguments drawn from two areas: natural science and a reading of Hegel's idea of freedom as a 'struggle for recognition'. The first, he claims, makes necessary 'a universal evolution in the direction of capitalism' (1992: xv). Fukuyama explains this necessity in the following way:

> The unfolding of modern natural science has had a uniform effect on all societies that have experienced it, for two reasons. In the first place, technology confers decisive military advantages on those countries that possess it. . . . Second, modern natural science establishes a uniform horizon of economic production possibilities. Technology makes possible the limitless accumulation of wealth, and thus the satisfaction of an ever-expanding set of human desires. This process guarantees an increasing homogenisation of all human societies, regardless of their origins or cultural inheritances.
>
> (1992: xiv)

What he is suggesting here is that the development of new technologies is a cumulative process which confers both a military and an economic advantage on the society that generates them. Moreover, the globalisation of trade that technological development permits erases the differences between cultures as their citizens strive to purchase the same international brands. Because, for Fukuyama, capitalism is best able to provide the conditions for this development its spread to all corners of the world is guaranteed.

The second strand in Fukuyama's argument is necessary because he has to prove a connection between capitalism and liberal democracy. As he admits, while 'modern natural science guides us to the gates of the Promised Land of liberal democracy, it does not deliver us to the Promised Land itself, for there is no economically necessary reason why industrialisation should produce political liberty' (1992: xv). This leads him to explore the idea of society as a 'struggle for recognition' in an argument that is based loosely on Hegel's discussion in the *Phenomenology of Spirit*. Fukuyama argues that freedom is constituted not only by the opening of markets so that everyone can purchase whatever is needed to satisfy their needs but it also rests upon the subject's desire to be 'recognised as a *human being*, that is, a being with a certain worth or dignity' (1992: xvi). He claims that this desire for recognition is resolved in liberal democracy because it is based on equality: every member of such a society, irrespective of how rich or poor they might be, has an equal right to vote to determine the form of government under which they live. On the basis of this, Fukuyama concludes that the reconciliation of the struggle for recognition in liberal democracy provides the 'missing link between liberal economics and liberal politics' (1992: xviii). In short, with free-market liberalism, the West has achieved a rational system that is capable of reconciling within itself any contradiction that might arise.

So has history ended in the realisation of the modern project of universal freedom? This certainly does not seem to be in keeping with Lyotard's or Jameson's analyses that were examined earlier in this book. Is the sort of postmodern theory introduced so far therefore irrelevant? Fukuyama's argument might seem immediately falsifiable on the basis of empirical evidence such as the growing inequality between rich and poor, the fact that in Britain and America fewer and fewer people bother to exercise their democratic rights, the illiberality of our treatment of refugees trying to enter the West, or even the occurrence of particular events such as the terrorist attacks on the USA on 11 September 2001. His argument anticipates such an objection, however, by claiming that despite the challenges that liberal democracy faces, 'these problems are not obviously insoluble on the basis of liberal principles, nor so serious that they would lead to the collapse of society as a whole, as communism collapsed in the 1980s' (1992: xxi). In other words, for the critic who believes Fukuyama's premise that his version of liberal democracy is the 'ideal' form of social organisation that 'could not be improved upon', this sort of empirical evidence will in no way serve to refute his argument.

The French philosopher Jacques Derrida takes another tack. Noting the evangelical tone of Fukuyama's writing, which presents his argument as the 'good news' (Fukuyama, 1992: xiii) and depicts liberal democracy as the 'Promised Land' (xv), Derrida argues that he substitutes 'an *ideal* good news' for the 'empirically observable event' of the end of history in a way that draws attention to the gap between reality and Fukuyama's rational system: 'the gap between fact and ideal essence does not show up only in . . . so-called primitive forms of government, theocracy and military dictatorship' but also characterises '*all* democracies, including the oldest and most stable of so-called Western democracies' (Derrida, 1994: 64). In other words, for Derrida the invocations of Christian salvation are employed to cover up a constitutive gap in Fukuyama's argument, which is based on a split between the idealisation of liberal democracy and the free market and the impossibility of demonstrating that such a system can actually exist in the way he claims. To return to Hegel, it would seem that Fukuyama misses the central premise of the dialectic: the philosophical reconciliation of rationality and reality is replaced in *The End of History* by a faith-based case that the 'Promised Land' is but a step away and the problems that we face are the last gasps of contradictions that are already resolved. Despite Fukuyama's claims, his argument is not a fulfilment of Hegel's philosophy but a retreat from it to a pre-Hegelian faith in salvation.

In direct contrast to this, Baudrillard's analysis of the postmodern presents contemporary culture as a perverse literalisation of Hegel's argument about the relation between the actual and the rational in what he calls the 'hyperreal':

> There is no longer any critical and speculative distance between the real and the rational. There is no longer really even any projection of models in the real . . . but an in-the-field, here-and-now transfiguration of the real into model. A fantastic short-circuit: the real is hyperrealised. Neither realised nor idealised: but hyperrealised. The hyperreal is the abolition of the real not by violent distinction, but by its assumption, elevation to the strength of the model.
>
> (1983b: 83–4)

The postmodern, according to Baudrillard's analysis, marks the point at which the real has been entirely replaced and 'transfigured' by rationalised models and, as a result of this, the possibility of a 'critical and speculative distance' between them has collapsed. If, as Hegel argues, the progress of history is the development of a rational grasp of reality, Baudrillard claims that this process is completed in postmodern hyperreality and that history has therefore run its course. The effect of this, however, is very different from Hegel's idea of the realisation of universal freedom or Fukuyama's 'good news' about liberal democracy. Instead, it marks a loss of critical distance: we can no longer use reason to map the real because, due to the precision and complexity of our models, the two have become identical. What Baudrillard means by this is that with the advent of new sciences and technologies, the models that can be produced to understand the world have become more real, more sophisticated and more accurate than reality itself. Humanity has become lost in a realm of hyperreality that refuses us the distance to stand back from our experiences and question them; refuses us, in other words, a sense of historical perspective. If this is the end of history, it marks a particularly bleak denouement.

Baudrillard's analysis of the hyperreality of contemporary history is set out in the most sustained way in his book *The Illusion of the End* (1994). Here he argues that with the acceleration of change and transformation during the course of modernity we have now reached a point at which things happen too quickly to make sense:

> the acceleration of modernity, of technology, of events and media, of all exchanges – economic, political and sexual – has propelled us to 'escape velocity', with the result that we have flown free of the referential sphere of the real and of history.
>
> (1994: 1)

He claims that a 'degree of slowness', a 'degree of distance' and a 'degree of liberation' are required to 'bring about the kind of condensation or significant crystallisation of events we call history' (1994: 1), and that these have been lost in contemporary hyperreal culture.

The reason for this, according to Baudrillard, is that the increasing rapidity of communications technology information and exchange has caused the events that form the basis of historical narrative to become so over-determined by competing meanings, explanations and appropriations that they can no longer be subsumed within a particular system or grand narrative. The explosion of multiple sources and channels of competing interpretations, each of which strives to be the fastest, most accessible and enticing for the public, pushes the events themselves into the background so that the question of what they really involve, what really happened, becomes impossible to answer and, strictly speaking, irrelevant to the communication media. The events themselves, Baudrillard claims, have gone on strike:

> History has gradually narrowed down to the field of its probable causes and effects, and, even more recently, to the field of current events – its effects 'in real time'. Events now have no more significance than their anticipated meaning, their programming and their broadcasting. Only *this event strike* constitutes a true historical phenomenon – this refusal to signify anything whatever, or this capacity to signify anything at all. This is the true end of history, the end of historical Reason.
>
> (1994: 21–2)

What Baudrillard is presenting here is a version of the postmodern that recalls the earlier arguments of thinkers such as Jameson and Ihab Hassan who were discussed earlier. This postmodernism is a world of images whose referents have disappeared, a play of surfaces and effects as the media compete for the sexiest, most up-to-the-minute 'real-time' reports, a playful and depthless world that has lost critical distance from its sources in the pastiches and ironies of contemporary programming and broadcasting. The stuff of history has become another commodity to be bought by the spectator: packaged by media companies, one can tune in to virtual recreations of past ages and marvel at the computer-generated effects, experience the thrills of 'walking with dinosaurs', or rewrite history as one replays the great battles of the past as computer-game simulations, even having the 'honour' of being given a medal by Hitler at a ceremony recreated in black and white archive footage (for 'authenticity', of course) if one saves the Third Reich from Allied invasion during the Second World War (for a detailed discussion of the production of 'counterfactual histories' in computer games see Atkins, 2003: 86–110). Likening these sorts of representation to the development of more and more sophisticated and realistic recording technology in the music industry, Baudrillard claims that we strive everywhere to find 'the same stereophonic effect, the same effect of absolute proximity to the real, the same effect of simulation' (1994: 6), forgetting the music that was the reason for this process of innovation in the first place.

The outcome of this is that 'history itself has to be regarded as a chaotic formation, in which acceleration puts an end to linearity and the turbulence created by acceleration deflects history definitively from its end' (Baudrillard, 1994: 111), so that even posing the question of 'what is the meaning of the end of history?' becomes impossible. Not only has history ended, it has ended in an 'illusion' in which the apparent fullness, reality and immediacy of meaning provided by the contemporary media hides the fact that it is meaning itself that has been lost.

The question this raises, though, is what room for criticism are we left with? This is difficult to answer. Baudrillard seems to suggest that any attempt to challenge the hyperreality of the present will always already have been undermined by the systems of simulation in which we live. In contrast to Fukuyama, whose inability to reconcile rationality in the form of liberal democracy with reality leads to a politics of faith, Baudrillard's collapsing of the real into the rationality of the hyperreal leaves, according to some commentators, little space either for faith or for hope as we get 'lost in the funhouse' of postmodernism (see Norris, 1990: 164–93).

Baudrillard does, however, hint at a critical stance towards the end of history in the final parts of *The Illusion of the End*, in which he suggests a movement from traditional forms of thinking about history to a more imaginative, literary mode that makes use of a range of poetic devices to present history differently:

> an anagrammatic history (where meaning is dismembered and scattered to the winds . . .), rhyming forms of political action or events which can be read in either direction . . . history lends itself to such a poetic convulsion, to such a subtle form of return and anaphora which, like the anagram, would – beyond meaning – allow the pure materiality of language to show through. . . . Such would be the enchanted alternative to the linearity of history, the poetic alternative to the disenchanted confusion, the chaotic profusion of present events.
>
> (1994: 122)

What this poetic form of history might look like is left undisclosed in Baudrillard's writing. There are, however, other postmodern thinkers who explore the possibility of a literary presentation of history in more detail.

FINITE HISTORY AND HISTORY AS NARRATIVE

For Aristotle the relation between history and poetry is one of opposition as the focus on particularity in the former is defined as entirely distinct from the universality of the latter. For Sidney, the opposition lies between history and moral philosophy, with poetry as a potential site of mediation. According to modern writers such as Hegel or Scott the aim is to produce a universal history by synthesising the potentials of these forms. Instead of synthesis, however, postmodern theorists and authors frequently tend to play them off against each other to produce complex configurations that resist both separation and synthesis. In postmodernist historical theory, the focus frequently falls on the act of writing history, and the social and political questions evoked by different narrative strategies: what are the relations and differences between literary and historical forms? Who is able to write history? In whose voice is it written? How can it be rewritten? What are the philosophical and political implications of particular historical forms and structures?

In an important essay entitled 'Finite History', Jean-Luc Nancy asks what sort of historical writing might be possible at the point at which the modern grand narratives have ceased to function and 'history is suspended, or even finished, as *sense*, as the directional and teleological path that it has been considered to be since the beginning of modern historical thinking' (1993: 144). Nancy argues that with the collapse of the grand narratives of modern history the world no longer has a sense that can be determined and mapped as a universal structure:

> There is no longer any world: no longer a *mundus*, a *cosmos*, a composed and complete order (from) within which one might find a place, a dwelling, and the elements of an orientation. . . . There is no longer any Spirit of the world, nor is there any history before whose tribunal one could stand.
>
> (1997: 4)

The modern grand narratives, such as Hegel's speculative dialectic or Scott's historical novels, generated a sense of the world, an explanation of identity and an idea of universal ethical and political responsibility. But these, argues Nancy, have vanished. In place of this universal history, the postmodern presents multiple, conflicting, 'finite' histories. No longer presented as the story of the grand, the infinite, progress of mankind from creation to salvation, history splits into multiple versions and narrative types that are generated by the needs and desires of particular communities whose conflicting ideals can never be reconciled in a universal system. The focus in these sorts of history falls, according to Nancy, on 'historicity as performance' (1993: 144), or, in other words, on the idea that through its histories a community presents to itself a sense of its identity and togetherness, a catalogue of its struggles and triumphs, and an account of its differences from other groups and factions. What becomes important on this account is the *way* in which a particular history is written, the *story* it tells.

The American historian and theorist Hayden White prepares the ground for some versions of postmodern historiography when he investigates history as text, or, in other words, in terms of the attributes that history writing borrows from literature. He argues that all history writing employs 'emplotment': 'the encodation of the facts contained in the chronicle as components of specific kinds of plot structures' (White, 1978: 83). Histories, he argues, take the form of narratives, and the ways in which the events described are portrayed, linked and made sense of are themselves susceptible to critical interrogation: 'histories ought never to be read as unambiguous signs of events they report, but rather as symbolic structures, extended metaphors, that "liken" the events reported in them to some form with which we have already become familiar in our literary culture' (1978: 91). What White is getting at here is that historical events do not mean things in themselves but, rather, their meanings are generated by the ways in which they are described and linked together to form a historical narrative, and the resonances produced by that narrative depend on the recognition by its audience of the familiar story-telling devices it employs. This, of course, has always been the case with history writing, but in the absence of a belief in the validity of modernity's grand narratives our perception of the focus of historical analysis changes:

> a specifically *historical* inquiry is born less of the necessity to establish *that* certain events occurred than of the desire to determine what certain events might *mean* for a given group, society, or culture's conception of its present tasks and further prospects.
>
> (White, 1986: 487)

This leads, White argues, to a sense of 'historical pluralism' (1986: 480) in which different groups' or cultures' accounts of a historical event cannot simply be ruled true or false on the basis of their relationship to a grand narrative, but rather require different sorts of analysis that explore their philosophical, political and literary underpinnings. History ceases to be a great, universal story of human progress and becomes a field of conflict where different interests and narratives interweave with and question each other.

It is not, however, quite as simple as this account of an apparently free play of different historical narratives suggests. The contemporary world remains full of universalising narratives, structures and organisations that range from the resurgence in religious fundamentalisms and the global campaigns of multinational companies to Fukuyama's liberal democracy and George Bush senior's 'New World Order' that was declared after the first Gulf War. Each of these rests upon ideas of humanity, freedom and progress that trace their lineages back to the sort of philosophy that the discussion of Hegel introduced. The grand narratives of modernity, albeit often in different forms from earlier times, still exert a huge influence on contemporary culture. This means that the task of the postmodern historian or writer of finite history is not simply to make up new stories but to interrogate the universal assumptions of our contemporary power structures, to challenge their explanatory schemes and make room for different voices to emerge. The urgency of these challenges is most readily identifiable in the work of feminist and postcolonial writers who question the exclusion of women and non-Europeans from traditional accounts of the past.

A key example of this sense of postmodern history as a challenge to the exclusive structures of a grand narrative might be located in the postcolonial theory of Homi Bhabha, who argues that the 'struggle against colonial oppression not only changes the direction of Western history, but challenges its historicist idea of time as a progressive, ordered whole' (Bhabha, 1994: 41). What he means by this is that postcolonialism's struggle against the grand narratives that underpin imperialist thought is not based simply on a strategy of 'changing' their 'direction' to include under the heading 'Man' people from non-European or North American cultures, but that it is also seeking to transform the idea of progress and universality by thinking about the discontinuities generated by the violence of colonialism. On the basis of this, a key aim of Bhabha's criticism is to produce counter-narratives that make explicit the legacies and effects of the carnage and brutality of colonial rule that modern histories have tended to downplay.

Similarly, the French feminist Julia Kristeva describes the importance of transforming modern approaches to history so as to take account of the politics of gender. Feminist historiography, she argues, must follow a twofold strategy of exploring both women's '*insertion* into history and the radical *refusal* of the subjective limitations imposed by this history's time on an experiment carried out in the name of . . . irreducible difference' (Kristeva, 1989: 198). Modern feminism, she claims, follows the first path by way of a universalising approach that 'inserts' women back into the grand narratives of history on the basis of a claim for equal rights: 'this current in feminism *globalises* the problems of women . . . under the label "Universal Woman"' (1989: 197) whose equality with 'Universal Man' must be asserted. In contrast to this, the second (more recognisably postmodern) approach, 'by demanding recognition of an irreducible identity, without equal in the opposite sex and, as such, exploded, plural, fluid, in a certain way nonidentical . . . situates itself outside the linear time of identities' (1989: 198). In other words, it breaks with the grand narrative structures to explore the ways in which the inherent plurality of female subjectivity subverts the identity politics of universalism and also the idea of a linear historical progression. For Kristeva, then, the exploration of what she calls 'women's time' aims to produce histories capable of recognising the presence of women in the past while refusing to mythologise 'Woman' as an abstract universal category. The result of this would again be a multiplicity of histories that explore the ways in which the differences within and between the sexes have been controlled, denied or suppressed by patriarchal societies.

RE-IMAGINING HISTORY: POSTMODERN FICTION

Besides opening up history to the possibility of a wide range of counter-narratives, the postmodern focus on the politics of narrative construction in the writing of history also makes room for a challenge to the sort of historical novel that follows on from Scott. As the discussion of Gray's

Poor Things in Chapter 1 set out to demonstrate, postmodern fiction frequently treats history ironically as a site of fragmentation rather than a progressive structure. This reworking of history, which Hutcheon names 'historiographic metafiction', can be seen in the work of a wide range of contemporary writers, each of whom draws from a different community and uses a different set of literary devices to question the traditional methods of historical representation for a different set of ends. Employing such devices as unreliable narrators, multiple frames for the narrative, stylistic transformations, mixtures of magical and realistic events, and parodies of earlier literary and historical works, this sort of postmodern fiction sets out to challenge traditional ideas of narrative construction, verisimilitude and historical truth.

A disturbing example of the use of an unreliable narrator to challenge the recognised historical record can be found in the figure of Oskar Matzerath from Günter Grass's trilogy of novels, first published in German between 1959 and 1963, about the Polish town Danzig (now renamed Gdansk): *The Tin Drum, Cat and Mouse*, and *Dog Years*. Oskar, who narrates the first of these novels and appears as a minor character in the other two, tells the story of his youth from a room in a mental hospital. We thus see the Nazi invasion of Poland and its recapture by the Russians through the eyes of a childlike figure who obsessively beats a tin drum, whose screams break glass and who, we are told, 'decided' to stop growing at the age of three when he threw himself down the cellar steps. Unlike Edward Waverley, Oskar is anything but an Everyman figure: his actions during the novel, which range from disrupting a Nazi rally with his drumming to manning the German defences on the Channel coast, and his sardonic descriptions of the characters and events of the Second World War provide little in the way of a trustworthy account of historical progress. As a narrator, he is mendacious, partial and far from sane. The view of history that is presented by the novel is thus by turns amusing, disturbing, macabre and outrageous: the violent swings of mood in the writing evoke the violence of the transformations that Danzig/Gdansk was forced to undergo during the twentieth century, and the insanity of the novel's narrator echoes the wider social unrest and madness of the period.

The use of multiple narrative frames and styles that continually force the reader to reassess the truth of what is happening in the story was introduced in the discussion of McHale's idea of the postmodern novel as dominated by ontological uncertainty in Chapter 1. Many of the plays by the contemporary British dramatist Peter Barnes employ just this technique of mixing dramatic styles and continually disturbing the narrative flow to explore the links between well-known historical events and the present. In *Red Noses*, first performed by the Royal Shakespeare Company in 1985, he depicts the Black Death and the struggles that emerged between the established church, religious fundamentalists and a newly emergent merchant class as each group sought to take control during the breakdown of social order. In the midst of this, a group of jesters attempts to use laughter to ease the suffering. Equally, in a play from 1978 called *Laughter*, Barnes explores the relation between comedy and violence through the depictions of Ivan the Terrible's torture chambers and the boredom of office work as a group of civil servants while away the hours as they send Jews to the gas chambers. In both of these plays, the mixture of theatrical styles (both inter-cut between realism, melodrama, tragedy and farce at regular intervals), the bizarre juxtapositions of characters and events (the petty jealousies of an office side by side with the organisation of the Final Solution), anachronism, magic and humour are employed to evoke striking parallels between historical events and those of contemporary society while raising complex questions for the audience about how it should respond.

Although not necessarily dealing directly with historical events, the use of parodies of earlier works of art or literature also sheds some light on the transformative potential of postmodern narrative and the problems of historical representation. The South African author J.M. Coetzee's *Foe*, first published in 1986, rewrites Daniel Defoe's eighteenth-century novel *Robinson Crusoe* in a way that brings to the surface many of the earlier work's colonial assumptions. In *Foe* a female narrator, Susan Barton, is cast away on a desolate island where she meets Cruso [*sic*] and his tongueless slave Friday. Having been rescued, Cruso dies and she returns to England with Friday to find someone to tell her story, happening upon the rather disreputable author Daniel Foe. The novel charts the struggle between Barton and Foe over how to narrate her experiences (she wants him to write a 'true history', he insists upon making it an exciting story – the story, we might suppose, of *Robinson Crusoe*), and their attempts to get Friday to speak. Entirely mute, Friday becomes the central gap around which the conflict between history and fiction revolves. In an important passage, Barton argues,

> Friday has no command of words and therefore no defence against being re-shaped day by day in conformity with the desires of others. I say he is a cannibal and he becomes a cannibal; I say he is a laundryman and he becomes a laundryman. What is the truth of Friday? You will respond: he is neither cannibal nor laundryman, these are mere names, they do not touch his essence, he is a substantial body, he is himself, Friday is Friday. But that is not so. No matter what he is to himself (is he anything to himself? – how can he tell us?), what he is to the world is what I make of him.
>
> (Coetzee, 1987: 121–2)

The problem here, of speaking for others who cannot represent themselves, whose desires and self-images are unknowable, is crucial to a postmodern thinking of history. What Coetzee's novel brings to the fore are the political problems inherent in the representation of other cultures, peoples and periods in history. Friday is a figure who fractures the novel's narrative by making impossible a reconciliation between Barton's history and Foe's fiction: for the former, he is an absence, a gap in which the possibility of 'telling the truth' breaks down due to lack of evidence; for the latter, his absolute passivity and apparent lack of desire or motivation make him impossible to characterise as anything other than an inert object. In this way *Foe* illustrates a central premise of Hutcheon's notion of postmodern narrative: historiographic metafiction, she argues, 'keeps distinct its formal auto-representation and its historical context, and in doing so problematises the very possibility of historical knowledge, because there is no reconciliation, no dialectic here – just unresolved contradiction' (1988: 106).

Each in its own way, these examples of postmodern literature all produce alternative forms of history to those of the modern grand narrative. They work to raise questions for contemporary audiences about the historical and social traditions that organise the cultural and political discourse that shapes the present. But what are the social and political consequences of this questioning? As Hamilton argues,

> An alternative history has to imagine an alternative society as well. . . .
> Disaffection with continuity, tradition and accredited forms of trans-
> mitting the past stretches through the critic of modernity to become the
> main source of postmodern discontent . . .
>
> (1996: 209)

A question often levelled at the postmodern writer or critic picks up on
the problem of this alternative: if this reworking of history is to have any
value, how does it help one figure or construct an alternative present?
Or, put simply, can there be a productive politics outside of the grand
narratives of modernity? This will be the subject of the next chapter.

5

POLITICS

If the progressive universal development of history and the idea of the subject, the agent of change, have been as thoroughly disrupted as the last two chapters have argued, what is left? In the light of these critiques, can there still be a productive postmodern politics? Many of its detractors are keen to argue that there cannot.

The death of postmodernism has been announced more than once. Most recently, the attack on the World Trade Center on 11 September 2001 marked, for some thinkers, its last rites and final burial. A widely discussed article published in *Time Magazine* a fortnight after the event sees the destruction as marking the beginning of a new realism:

> One good thing could come from this horror: it could spell the *end of the age of irony*. For some 30 years – roughly as long as the Twin Towers were upright – the good folks in charge of America's intellectual life have insisted that nothing was to be believed in or taken seriously. Nothing was real. . . . The consequence of thinking that nothing is real – apart from prancing around in an air of vain stupidity – is that one will not know the difference between a joke and a menace. No more. The planes that plowed into the World Trade Center and the Pentagon were real. The flames, smoke, sirens – real. The chalky landscape, the silence of the streets – all real.
>
> (Rosenblatt, 2001: 79)

The argument here, that postmodernism's loss of a sense of the 'real world' makes it a dangerously reactionary critical formation that must be replaced, is not a new one. It is not even one that has been attached only to major international disasters or conflicts. Rather, for those who set out to challenge postmodern theory, practically every aspect of postmodernism and postmodernity has been seen as a viable target.

According to its many detractors, postmodernism is a spoilt teenager, solipsistically obsessed with its own self-image as arbiter of the latest fads and fashions from across the range of recent culture. This attitude is manifested in the vagaries of a contemporary art scene that has lost all touch with the day-to-day realities and concerns of the general public. In media studies, a discipline that could (and might) have been made for the postmodernist, the recent fascination with cyberspace, cyborgs and cybernetics that looks forward to a future in which the differences between humans and machines have begun to efface themselves seems to demand that we forget entirely the more than a billion people in the world who have no access to clean water and electricity, let alone the world wide web. Just as women, gays and minority peoples from across the globe begin to step forward to assert their identities, the postmodernist attempts to pull the rug from under their feet by claiming that identity is no more than an illusory construct that can be transformed at will through parodic performance. Turning its back on real-world problems to play games with intertextuality, hyperreality, indeterminacy and simulations of simulations which spiral off into the void without ever touching down on Earth, postmodernity has nothing of value to say about the collapse of traditional communities in the face of globalisation and the ever-widening gap between the haves and the have-nots. The world seems to be becoming more dangerous every minute as the violent fundamentalists of the Middle East and Mid West face off, murdering each other's citizens with barbaric terrorist atrocities or the horrific and irresistible force of the long-range bomber and 'precision' missile strike. But what does the postmodern critic have to say about any of this? One so-called postmodernist has reportedly claimed that the Gulf War, which played a key part in creating the current world climate, 'did not take place' (Baudrillard, 1995). For another, apparently, history has reached the concluding stage of its evolution in liberal democracy, and this means that all opposition to US hegemony is wrong-headed and ephemeral

(Fukuyama, 1992). The postmodern, for all its complex jargon and high-flown rhetoric, is incapable of responding adequately to the most pressing issues that confront the world today. The postmodernist, these critics might claim, would fiddle while the world burned if it were not for the fact that he or she had traded in the old-fashioned stringed instrument for the drum machines and samplers that are the stuff of contemporary popular music.

All of the arguments in the preceding paragraph have been hurled at the postmodern during the last decade or two, some of them even hitting the mark. There are certainly postmodern critics who have held positions not much more sophisticated than those caricatured above. However, those who clamour for the demise of postmodern theory frequently miss the range of vital insights provided by a variety of thinkers who are not content with simplistic celebrations of free play and hyperreality. I do not want to end this book with an argument that purports to reveal 'what's wrong with postmodernism' (Norris, 1990) or to sound its death knell in the aftermath of the events of 11 September 2001. Rather, what follows aims to demonstrate the importance and vitality of postmodern theory by putting the case that many of its critics have failed to grasp the radical political and philosophical potential that the postmodern is able to attain in the work of the more astute contemporary writers who have come to prominence under the postmodern banner. This chapter thus has two basic tenets. The first is that, despite the clamour of its conservative critics, in our rapidly changing world, the challenges that confront critical thinking might best be understood with ideas drawn from postmodern theory. The second, that if these challenges are to be met, what is needed is a critically and theoretically rigorous idea of the postmodern that acknowledges the complexities of its modern intellectual and cultural heritage while, at the same time, identifying precisely the reasons for its deviations from that past.

As the discussions included in this book have suggested, the relation between postmodernism and contemporary capitalism has been both very close and extremely fraught. For many postmodern theorists, capitalism marks the new globalised horizon of contemporary culture: there is no longer anywhere outside it where one can stand, no straightforward alternative to it that one can champion, and yet its effects must be resisted as they are potentially devastating – politically, socially, culturally and ecologically. And yet, as the supporters of international free trade frequently tell us, there is no workable alternative to its worldwide networks of finance and exchange. Postmodern economic globalisation thus shatters the modern projects of organisation, welfare and nationhood. As social theorist Ulrich Beck puts it,

> In this pitch-dark view of things, economic globalisation merely completes what has been driven forward intellectually by postmodernism and politically by individualisation: namely, the collapse of modernity. The diagnosis points towards a *capitalism without work* that will *create unemployment on a huge scale*; the historical association between market economy, welfare state and democracy, the Western model that integrated and legitimated the nation-state project of modernity, is thus destined to break down.
>
> (Beck, 2000: 100)

This is not, for Beck, the replacement of the many sovereign nations by a single world power but rather a process in which a 'globally *disorganised* capitalism is continually spreading out' (2000: 103) as the ability of states to regulate their economies and distribute welfare to their citizens is eroded by the increasingly interconnected world markets in which finance and employment move quickly away from any society that seems likely to prove expensive. Since the fall of the Berlin wall in 1989 and the dissolution of the Soviet Union, communism, modernity's main model of opposition to capitalist economic and social organisation, seems rapidly to be disappearing: the East–West split between communism and capitalism that shaped the immediate post-Second World War era and the Cold War is being refigured in the face of new threats and challenges to generate a world that seems much more complex and fragmented. Thinkers such as Fukuyama have been quick to identify these events as proof of the 'good news' that free-market liberal democracy is the best and only form of contemporary politics. And, from the opposite perspective, the various groups who, despite their differences, have come together to protest against globalisation and contemporary capitalism have done so without a coherent sense of an alternative world order.

But what is capitalism? In its broadest sense, the term takes in those economic systems in which privately held finance is used for the production, purchase and consumption of goods, and has been the basic economic model for a vast range of societies stretching back to the earliest cultures. In the words of the eighteenth-century Scottish economist and philosopher Adam Smith in his extremely influential book from 1776, *The Wealth of Nations*, capitalism is an inevitable aspect of human being and interaction: it emerges from 'a certain propensity in human nature . . . the propensity to truck, barter, and exchange one thing for another' (Smith, 1986: 117). Although Smith is uninterested in 'Whether this propensity be one of the original principles in human nature . . . or whether, as seems more probable, it be the necessary consequence of the faculties of reason and speech' (1986: 117–18), he is certain that it stands as the basis of all human culture. It has manifested itself in a vast number of different ways in different societies, and has been the subject of much debate and conflict, but for Smith it is the economic system that best expresses who we are.

Although thinkers such as Smith trace its origins back to the dawn of civilisation, the term only really comes into its modern usage at the beginning of the nineteenth century when it is employed to define the growth of industrial production, the expansion of markets and the employment of workers by businesses for wages rather than a share of the produce of their labour. And it is in opposition to this modern understanding that the most important critical analysis of and challenge to capitalism is issued by Karl Marx (1818–83).

MODERN POLITICS AND CRITIQUE: MARX

If the desubstantialisation of the human subject and the dialectical, progressive development of history are two of modernity's most central tenets, a third is the argument that the conditions that hold in a given society are always open to critique and transformation. As the discussion of Habermas in Chapter 2 indicated, the discourse of modernity has always been critical: almost all of the thinkers, artists and writers who are gathered under its banner by contemporary critics tend to view their work as providing alternatives to their own present-day realities. If, on the one hand, modern thought seeks to understand what modernity is and how the world works, it also, on the other hand, aims to question, challenge and transform it. This attitude towards reality is summed up most succinctly by Marx, who argues that, 'The philosophers have only inter-preted the world, in various ways; the point is to change it' (Marx, 2000: 173). It is important to note here that Marx is not advocating a with-drawal from understanding in favour of practical action. Rather, what he is making a case for is a practical philosophy that seeks, through understanding the world differently, the means to mobilise the people to transform it.

As an example of the ways in which the discourse of modernity might be at the same time an attempt to understand the world and also to change it, I want to explore Marx's critique of capitalism in some more detail. This is not because his idea of communism is the only form of critical modernity. It is not. Thinkers such as Smith, Descartes, Kant and Hegel each produced critiques that engage with the politics of their times and, albeit in very different ways and for different ends, seek to produce what they see as more rational and just worlds. Marxism is, however, one of the most sustained, rigorous and revolutionary political analyses of modern society, and is also perhaps the most influential on postmodern thought.

So what is the basis of Marx's account of society and politics? What is at stake in his critique of capitalism? If we are to have any understanding of the way in which Marx has influenced and been opposed by postmodern thinkers, a brief outline of his philosophy will help to set the scene.

Marx set out in the second half of the nineteenth century to challenge the dehumanising effects of what he saw as an inherently self-contradictory capitalist society:

> In our days everything seems pregnant with its contrary. Machinery, gifted with the wonderful power of shortening and fructifying human labour, we behold starving and overworking it. The new-fangled sources of wealth, by some strange weird spell, are turned into sources of want. The victories of art seem bought by the loss of character. At the same time that mankind masters nature, man seems to become enslaved to other men or by his own infamy. Even the pure light of science seems to shine on the dark background of ignorance. . . . In the signs that bewilder the middle class, the aristocracy and the poor prophets of regression, we do recognise our brave friend . . . the Revolution.
>
> (Marx, 2000: 368–9)

Marx's analysis of his times sets out to demonstrate the contradictions inherent in nineteenth-century capitalism. In response to these, and in keeping with the processes of modern forms of critique, he sets up an alternative revolutionary grand narrative in opposition to the prevalent grand narratives, and most particularly that of capitalism, that governed the societies of Europe in the aftermath of the Industrial Revolution. This grand narrative might be called historical materialism.

Marx's historical materialism takes its central premises from Hegel, by whom the young Marx was hugely influenced, but turns Hegel's speculative dialectic (which was introduced in Chapter 4) on its head to replace the earlier thinker's idealism with a materialist analysis of reality that takes economic and political forces as the bases that shape experience. According to Marx, although Hegel's dialectic correctly diagnoses the fact that progress occurs through conflict and contradiction, it dwells too much in the realm of abstract ideas and fails to grasp the influence that the material world has on both individual thought and social interaction. In an argument that develops from the sort of modern account of subjectivity that we saw in Kant and Wordsworth in Chapter 3, Marx argues that identity and consciousness are not innate to subjects, but are generated by their material surroundings and, most importantly, their relations to others in society: 'It is not the consciousness of men that determines their being, but, on the contrary, their social being that determines their consciousness' (2000: 425). According to Marx, human consciousness (the 'I think') does not pre-exist and determine identity and social interaction. Rather, the consciousness that the 'I think' identifies is determined by the social context from which it emerges. A medieval peasant, for example, would have a fundamentally different sense of self and identity from a twenty-first-century stockbroker, a different perception of the world and different relations with others in society. Like Hegel, then, Marx's argument is that consciousness is culturally and historically determined. The difference between the grand narratives that the two thinkers produce rests on their different accounts of what generates social and historical change. For Hegel, spirit is the moving force of progress that works through the various stages of contradiction between reason and reality; according to Marx, conflict and contradiction take place not between reason and reality but within the material forces and institutions of economic production and consumption.

For Marx, it is the subject's position in relation to the economic structure of society that produces identity. He argues that,

> In the social production of their life, men enter into definite relations that are indispensable and independent of their will, relations of production which correspond to a definite stage of development of their material productive forces. The sum total of these relations of production constitutes the economic structure of society, the real foundation, on which rises a legal and political superstructure and to which correspond definite forms of social consciousness.
>
> (2000: 425)

The key claim made by this passage is that the consciousness of a given society and the identities of the subjects that make it up are founded on the ways in which that society produces the means by which it survives, or, in other words, on the basis of its economic organisation. Marx argues that the productive forces of a society, which might range from the peasant agriculture of the earliest cultures to the mines and factories of an industrial society or even to today's high-tech information-rich and technology-driven economies, generate certain sets of relations of production, by which he means certain forms of organisation and administration that allow production to occur. Consciousness of the world is determined by the subject's relations to the productive forces; so, for example, a worker in a factory will have a very different sense of society from the owner and manager of that factory: they will have very different opportunities in terms of wealth, education, legal rights and even life expectancy. This argument is often referred to as the 'base–superstructure' account of society: the productive forces and economic relations are the base on which the cultural superstructure (the arts, education, the law, family relations, etc.) stands, and determine the sorts of superstructural institutions and rules such a society will be capable of producing, as well as the identities of its subjects.

This analysis of the structures of identity and society forms the basis of Marx's materialist account of historical change and progress, and differentiates the Marxist grand narrative from the one produced by Hegel's speculative philosophy. The passage from his 1845 book, *The German Ideology*, which formulates this, is worth quoting at length:

This conception of history depends on our ability to expound the real process of production, starting out from the material production of life itself, and to comprehend the form of intercourse connected with this and created by this mode of production (i.e. civil society in its various stages) as the basis of all history. . . . It shows that history does not end by being resolved into 'self-consciousness' as 'spirit of the spirit', but that in it at each stage there is found a material result: a sum of productive forces, an historically created relation of individuals to nature and to one another, which is handed down to each generation from its predecessor; a mass of productive forces, capital funds and conditions, which, on the one hand, is indeed modified by the new generation, but also, on the other, prescribes for it its conditions of life and gives it a definite development, a special character. It shows that circumstances make men just as much as men make circumstances.

(Marx, 2000: 188–9)

Instead of focusing on the movement of spirit as the guiding force of development, Marx concentrates on the conflicts between different forms of economic organisation. These forms, he argues, determine the power to control their lives that each generation has, their access to wealth and the freedom they experience. The economic order 'prescribes' the 'conditions of life' for individuals as well as determining what sorts of civil institutions a society can support. This is not to say that life is entirely pre-determined by the economy. It is, however, to acknowledge the important effects that wealth can have across generations.

If we take seriously his analysis of the social and historical construction of identity, it should be clear that one's class (or, in other words, one's position in relation to the productive forces of society) is a crucial aspect of consciousness because it regulates the opportunities and choices to which one has access. *The Communist Manifesto* (1848), written in collaboration with his colleague Friedrich Engels, takes up this point and opens with the following argument:

The history of all hitherto existing society is the history of class struggles. Freeman and slave, patrician and plebeian, lord and serf, guild-master and journeyman, in a word, oppressor and oppressed, stood in constant opposition to one another, carried on an uninterrupted, now hidden,

> now open fight, a fight that each time ended, either in a revolutionary re-
> constitution of society at large, or the common ruin of the contending
> classes.
>
> (Marx and Engels, 1967: 79)

It is important not to underestimate the centrality of this claim to Marx's thought. History and social organisation are based on the struggle for power between the different social classes and proceed by a series of revolutionary conflicts as one set of relations is replaced by another. As the forces of production develop, new classes rise to positions of dominance, and others lose their power to control their lives. In Marx's time, the key conflict was between the bourgeoisie, the owners of the mines and factories and their parliamentary representatives, who had come to power during the Industrial Revolution, and the proletariat or working class: those who did not own the means of production but were paid wages for their labour. He argues that one of the central forces of modern capitalism is the bourgeoisie's need to accumulate 'surplus value' by paying their workers less than the economic value of what their labour produces, and thereby enriching themselves. The proletariat are, on the other hand, forced to subsist and subjected to the fluctuations of the markets in which a downturn could mean unemployment and destitution. They are treated not as individuals, but as commodities as their labour is bought and sold on the markets.

This notion of 'surplus value' points to a distinction that is a key premise of Marxist economics: the difference between 'use value' and 'exchange value'. Marx explains this difference in the following way in his most important exposition of economic theory, *Capital*, first published in 1867:

> Every useful thing, as iron, paper, etc., may be looked at from the two
> points of view: of quality and quantity. . . . The utility of a thing makes
> it a use-value. . . . A commodity, such as iron, corn, or a diamond,
> is therefore, so far as it is a material thing, a use-value, something use-
> ful. . . . Exchange-value [in contrast] presents itself as a quantitative
> relation, as the proportion in which values in use of one sort are
> exchanged for those of another sort.
>
> (2000: 458–9)

The use value of an object identifies its quality: its propensity to be used to satisfy particular human needs or desires. The exchange value of an object, which is measured in terms of quantity, indicates its value as something to be bought, sold or exchanged on the markets, and thus treats it as a commodity. Crucially for Marx's analysis of economics, there is no natural relation between the two values. Rather, exchange value is determined by the markets and becomes the basis of capitalism, the aim of which is to maximise the value derived from the creation and exchange of commodities – to generate surplus value.

On the basis of these analyses of value, identity, society and history, Marx produces an argument about the ways in which the injustices of capitalism can be overcome by the proletariat:

> Of all the classes that stand face to face with the bourgeoisie today, the proletariat alone is a really revolutionary class. . . . The proletarians cannot become masters of the productive forces of society, except by abolishing their own previous mode of appropriation. They have nothing of their own to fortify; their mission is to destroy all previous securities for, and insurances of, individual property.
>
> (Marx and Engels, 1967: 91–2)

In keeping with the form of a grand narrative, Marx's work produces an analysis of history, an account of the present, and, as this passage suggests, a projection of the future. The task that history has bequeathed to the proletariat, he argues, is to rise up and overthrow the capitalist organisation of society, to liberate the productive forces from their appropriation by the bourgeoisie, and issue in a new communist order in which the inequality and want that underpin capitalism will be abolished. The point here is not that the proletariat simply replace the bourgeoisie and reverse the class structure. Rather, the aim of Marx's philosophy is that class is abolished entirely in a free and equal society in which all are allowed to flourish, in which 'everyone is only a worker like everyone else', and the goods that are produced are distributed 'from each according to his ability, to each according to his needs' (2000: 615).

For postmodern theory, this grand narrative structure of Marxist thought is one of its most problematic aspects. As the Italian postmodernist philosopher Gianni Vattimo argues, in the face of the dissolution of universal history, Marx's projection of a future where 'work would be freed from its alienating characteristics because its products, once removed from the perverse cycle of commerce, would retain a fundamental identity with their producer' ends up having to define this future 'in terms of complex political mediations that end up rendering it problematic and that in the last analysis expose its mythic nature' (Vattimo, 1988: 22). With the loss of the historical grand narrative comes the loss of an ability to organise society into clearly defined class groupings and also the loss of a belief in the necessity of a given projection of the future. And it is this threefold loss that produces some of the most difficult problems for postmodern politics as well as being the basis of the most vociferous critiques levelled at postmodernism by those left-wing theorists who still wish to cling to the Marxist grand narrative.

POSTMODERNITY AND 'LATE CAPITALISM': JAMESON

The postmodern theorist who is most concerned with working through the Marxist heritage to keep alive the idea of an oppositional critique while also recognising the force of economic and social transformations in contemporary postmodernity is Fredric Jameson. In *Postmodernism, or, the Cultural Logic of Late Capitalism*, he argues that 'every position on postmodernism in culture – whether apologia or stigmatisation – is also at one and the same time, and *necessarily*, an implicitly or explicitly political stance on the nature of multinational capitalism today' (1991: 3). I have already introduced his theory of pastiche as a postmodernist cultural style in Chapter 1, but it might now be useful to contextualise this in his broader account of postmodernity that draws heavily on Marx's ideas of political economy and materialist critique. For Jameson, the sorts of postmodernism we have been discussing in art, literature and general culture emerge out of the transformations that have taken place in capitalism during the second half of the twentieth century. And, as the title of his book suggests, postmodernism is not just contemporaneous with this transformation of economic structures into what he calls 'late capitalism', it is its 'cultural logic'. In other words, according to the Marxist account of society that Jameson produces, the cultural superstructures of postmodernism are determined by a transformation of the economic basis of society in late-capitalist postmodernity. In still other words, as the economic organisation of Western society has developed, the culture that surrounds it has changed.

Jameson borrows the term 'late capitalism' from the economist Ernest Mandel, who splits the development of modern capitalism into three major periods: the first is that of market capitalism, which developed from the factories and workshops of the Industrial Revolution during the nineteenth century; the second is monopoly capitalism that emerged with the growth of the large-scale businesses that rapidly took over whole markets in particular areas at the end of the nineteenth and beginning of the twentieth century; and the third, late capitalism, marks the era of multinational corporations and deregulated markets in which trade barriers between different countries and areas have rapidly broken down (see Mandel, 1978). The first and, to a certain extent, the second phases of capitalism are the focus of Marx's modern critique, but, for many postmodern theorists, in late capitalism economic organisation has changed so radically that a new approach becomes necessary.

Jameson describes the effects of this third stage of capitalism in some detail at the beginning of *Postmodernism*. What marks its development, he argues,

> is not merely an emphasis on the emergence of new forms of business organisation (multinationals, transnationals) beyond the monopoly stage but, above all, a vision of a world capitalist system fundamentally distinct from the older imperialism . . . its features include the new international division of labour, a vertiginous new dynamic in international banking and the stock exchanges (including the enormous Second and Third World debt), new forms of media interrelationship (very much including transportation systems such as containerisation), computers and automation, the flight of production to advanced Third World areas, along with all the more familiar social consequences, including the crisis of traditional labour, the emergence of yuppies, and gentrification on a now global scale.
>
> (1991: xviii–xix)

For Jameson, late capitalism marks a new 'vision of world capitalism' in which the systems that governed the West's economies during the nineteenth and early twentieth centuries develop and spread throughout the world as borders are broken down and new markets are founded in previously unpenetrated areas. This process has spread rapidly since the Second World War with the establishment of institutions such as the World Trade Organisation, World Bank and International Monetary Fund that oversee trade, structure debt repayments by developing countries and impose sanctions on states that refuse to open their markets to competition. The internationalisation of trade has, as Jameson suggests, also led to a transformation of working life as industrial production has moved away from its nineteenth-century European and American centres to relocate in the developing world where salaries can be far lower and workers have more limited access to employment rights and protection, allowing goods to be produced and sold more cheaply, and leading to consumer booms in the West. More than this, with the new communications media and international transport infrastructures, contacts between different parts of the world have sped up exponentially so that information and ideas can pass around the globe almost in an instant, and goods and people are able to travel at hitherto unanticipated rates.

These changes in the economic and communicational structures of society have gone hand in hand with changes in the use of images to appeal to consumers, creating what Jameson identifies as a new postmodern aesthetic:

> What has happened is that aesthetic production today has become integrated into commodity production generally: the frantic economic urgency of producing fresh waves of ever more novel-seeming goods (from clothing to airplanes), at ever greater rates of turnover, now assigns an increasingly essential structural function and position to aesthetic innovation and experimentation.

> (1991: 4–5)

What Jameson is identifying here is the increase in the rapidity of changes of fashion that accompanies the development of advertising and makes consumption a matter not just of useful products but also of images and lifestyle choices. Rather than purchasing just objects, we now buy brands and identities in the shape of everything from cosmetic implants to designer ring tones for our mobile telephones. This, in turn, leads to what he calls a 'new depthlessness' (1991: 6) in which each commodity becomes just another interchangeable image or fashion accessory to be purchased by the consumer to enhance their choice of lifestyle.

As an image for this new depthlessness, Jameson contrasts two paintings: 'A Pair of Boots' by the Dutch modernist artist, Vincent Van Gogh, and 'Diamond Dust Shoes' by pop artist Andy Warhol. The former depicts a pair of battered boots caked in dust in a context, that of the agricultural life of the peasant who presumably owned them, and provides the viewer with a sense of the rural world from which they came. The latter, in contrast, presents a collection of women's shoes floating freely in space, and apparently also free from any social context whatsoever. According to Jameson, Warhol's painting

> no longer speaks to us with any of the immediacy of Van Gogh's footgear; indeed, I am tempted to say that it does not really speak to us at all. Nothing in this painting organises even a minimal place for the viewer . . . [It marks] a new kind of flatness or depthlessness, a new kind of superficiality in the most literal sense, perhaps the supreme formal feature of all the postmodernisms . . .
>
> (1991: 8–9)

As well as being an analysis of the works of art themselves, what Jameson is using this contrast to identify is the transformation of experience in postmodernity. The objects around us that we might once have experienced in terms of their use values are commodified to such an extent that exchange value, in fact the infinite exchangeability of all commodities, has come to account for the entirety of our experience of the world. Warhol's shoes are infinitely reproducible, interchangeable, superficial, and contextless, just one commodity from a potentially endless collection in which use value has become entirely irrelevant. This, Jameson argues, is the basis of the postmodern consumer culture that we inhabit.

According to Jameson, the primary experience of the depthlessness of postmodernity is akin to schizophrenia in which, cut off from any foundational context, the world 'comes before the subject with heightened intensity, bearing a mysterious charge of affect, here described in the negative terms of anxiety and loss of reality, but which one could just as well imagine in the positive terms of euphoria, a high, an intoxicatory or hallucinogenic intensity' (1991: 27–8). In other words, the transformation of social experience into an interchangeable flow of commodities in which everything is up for sale produces a loss of reality that is at once terrifying and euphoric. There is no longer any firm ground for experience as customs and traditions are continually cast aside with the advent of new fashionable lifestyle choices. We become no more than the sum total of our purchases, and the feeling associated with this is one of a 'heightened intensity' of experience suffused with a 'mystical charge' as it veers schizophrenically between intoxication and anxiety.

What concerns Jameson with all of this is the apparent lack of space for critique and resistance that postmodernity seems to offer. Trapped in its schizophrenic depthlessness, in which all objects from food to fashion have become interchangeable commodities, the traditional grounds of cultural context, custom, class and even family organisation have been swept from beneath our feet. The key task of the critic is to challenge this current late-capitalist status quo. As he says in another book, *The Geopolitical Aesthetic*, 'our most urgent task will be tirelessly to denounce the economic forms that have come for the moment to reign supreme and unchallenged' (1992: 212). What Jameson urges, then, is a rejection of late-capitalist consumer culture and an attempt to generate a postmodern version of critique that resists the depthless commodification of experience: a postmodern Marxism to challenge postmodern, or late, capitalism. In order to begin to formulate this, he proposes a process of what he describes as 'cognitive mapping', which 'involves the practical reconquest of a sense of place and the construction or reconstruction of an articulated ensemble which can be retained in memory and which the individual subject can map and remap along the moments of mobile, alternative trajectories' (1991: 51). As he acknowledges, it is impossible to return to a simpler, pre-late-capitalist state in which traditional relationships and forms of critique might avoid contemporary depthlessness. Instead, Jameson argues, critique must undertake a process of mapping that articulates the mass of objects and images that make up everyday life to 'enable a situational representation' of the subject's place within 'the vaster and properly unrepresentable totality which is the ensemble of society's structures as a whole' (1991: 51). What he is getting at here is the idea that, through analyses of particular cultural objects or structures, the critic should aim to produce accounts of how they emerge from, fit into and potentially disrupt the apparently universal systems of contemporary capitalism: generating a map that provides context and depth for the subject's experience of consumer culture. This mapping can be produced both by theory and, potentially, by postmodern art. Jameson concludes:

> the new political art (if it is possible at all) will have to hold to the truth of postmodernism, that is to say, to its fundamental object – the world of multinational capital – at the same time at which it achieves a breakthrough to some as yet unimaginable new mode of representing this last, in which we may again begin to grasp our positioning as individual and collective subjects and regain a capacity to act and struggle which is at present neutralised by our spatial as well as our social confusion. The political form of postmodernism, if there ever is any, will have as its vocation the invention and projection of a global cognitive mapping . . .

(1991: 54)

The tentative tone of this assertion ('if it is possible at all', 'if there ever is any') demonstrates the difficulty Jameson faces as a thinker who wants to retain the oppositional critical theory of his Marxist heritage and yet recognises the dissolution of the modern grand narratives and the difficulty of locating an 'outside' of global capitalism. A Marxist-style critique, in the form of cognitive mapping, remains possible, he claims, but the projection of a future in which the challenges of late capitalism have been resolved or even a concrete account of how collectively we might strive for it seem impossible.

POSTMODERN CONSUMPTION AND SIMULATION: BAUDRILLARD

If Jameson's prognosis of the possibilities of a modern form of political resistance is gloomy, it is Baudrillard's utter bleakness that has most upset left-leaning critics. His analyses of the postmodern share Jameson's sense that a loss of contact with reality has been generated by the recent transformations that have taken place in economics and communications technology. However, Baudrillard reacts to this in a very different way, and presses his conclusions much further and into far more controversial areas. A central tenet of his argument is that in contemporary culture, the object and the sign have become indistinguishable, and we have thereby replaced reality with simulation and the hyperreal. The basis of this loss of critical distance was introduced in terms of his analysis of history in Chapter 4, but it is worth developing that here to explore its relation to political theory and critique.

In one of his early books, *The Mirror of Production*, Baudrillard asserts that, today, 'capitalism crosses the entire network of natural, social, sexual and cultural forces, all languages and codes' (1975: 138). Contemporary capitalism, he argues, is not simply the circulation of money and commodities, but rather infests every aspect of experience. When one desires or purchases a commodity, one is not simply buying the object itself, but also the signs, images and identities that go along with it. In *The Consumer Society*, Baudrillard equates the commodity with the sign and argues that as they collapse into one another they generate the language or code that shapes postmodern identity:

> The circulation, purchase, sale, appropriation of differentiated goods and signs/objects today constitute our language, our code, the code by which the entire society *communicates* and converses. Such is the structure of consumption, its language, by comparison with which individual needs and pleasures are merely speech effects.
>
> (1998: 79–80)

Individual actions, on this view, are caught up with consumption, becoming statements in the language of capitalism. We are, for Baudrillard, what we consume, and this is tied up with our innermost desires. The postmodern consumer, he argues, 'sets in place a whole array of sham objects, of characteristic signs of happiness, and then waits . . . for happiness to alight' (1998: 31). The desire for happiness that underlies consumption is not, however, satisfied by any particular purchase; as the discussion of psychoanalysis in Chapter 3 argued, one always desires more, and this is adopted by Baudrillard as one of the moving principles of his theory. According to Rex Butler, an Australian Baudrillard scholar,

> consumption is not about matching a pre-existing desire to a particular set of objects. Rather . . . consumption is not possible without a certain

excess of desire over the object; or if desire is satisfied by the object, there is always another or an extra desire produced by this.

(Butler, 1999: 50)

For Baudrillard, the way in which this excess of desire is produced and manipulated in contemporary culture is the motivating force of capitalism and leads to the most central aspect of postmodernity: the ubiquity of the messages produced by advertising in the communications media and the subsequent annihilation of reality. This Baudrillard defines as the 'seduction' of the commodity (see Baudrillard, 1990).

According to Baudrillard, the contemporary mass media present a '*dizzying whirl of reality*' that is not a reflection of what 'really happens' in the 'real' world, but is rather a production of a simulated world in which 'we live, sheltered by signs, in the denial of the real' (1998: 34). Quite what he means by this might, at first, be difficult to grasp. However, in *Simulations*, the book that has often been described as Baudrillard's most central contribution to postmodern theory, he argues that the ubiquity of media representation has transformed the nature of appearance itself:

Three orders of appearance, parallel to the mutations of the law of value, have followed one another since the Renaissance:

– *Counterfeit* is the dominant scheme of the 'classical' period, from the Renaissance to the industrial revolution;
– *Production* is the dominant scheme of the industrial era;
– *Simulation* is the reigning scheme of the current phase that is controlled by the code.

The first order of simulacrum is based on the natural law of value, that of the second order on the commercial law of value, that of the third order on the structural law of value.

(1983a: 83)

Baudrillard presents a genealogy of the image here, which ties it to the development of modern capitalism. In the first order, appearance counterfeits reality as the image stands in for the real by representing it in its absence. So, for example, the portrait represents the person, and its value and truth rest on how lifelike that representation is. This is the familiar common-sense idea of the relation between image and reality: the former *represents* the latter for the thinking, independent Cartesian subject.

In the second order of appearance, which parallels the industrial organisation of modern capitalism, the value associated with an image changes: what becomes important is its ability to be bought and sold as images are no longer valued as copies of originals but in their own right. This is the order of mass production, and as Baudrillard argues, once images and things are produced on a gigantic scale, 'The relation between them is no longer that of an original to its counterfeit . . . but equivalence, indifference. In a series, objects become undefined simulacra one of the other' (1983a: 97). He is generalising here the insights about twentieth-century art that are developed in the work of the German cultural critic and philosopher Walter Benjamin (1892–1940). Benjamin argues in an influential essay entitled 'The Work of Art in the Age of Mechanical Reproduction' that with the emergence of forms such as photography and film the value of artworks ceases to be located in their authenticity or uniqueness and comes to be equated with an 'overcoming' of 'the uniqueness of every reality by accepting its reproduction' (Benjamin, 1973: 217). Due to the new technologies of the twentieth century, images become infinitely reproducible and, as Benjamin and Baudrillard agree, the focus moves from the representational authenticity of the unique image to the market-orientated politics of the mass media.

In the third order, which Baudrillard links to the postmodern, questions of originality and reality drop out altogether as images and objects become place-holders in a structural system in which all values have become entirely equivalent and exchangeable: we exist within an infinite code to which no one has the key. Baudrillard develops this idea of an infinite code of images within which the ideas of representation and reality have vanished from the French writer and revolutionary Guy Debord, who argued in his 1967 book, *The Society of the Spectacle*, that the 'whole life of those societies in which modern conditions of production prevail presents itself as an immense accumulation of *spectacles*. All that was once lived has become mere representation' with the result that spectacle 'epitomises the prevailing model of social life', the 'very heart of society's real unreality' (Debord, 2002: 12–13). Images and simulations become more immediate, more apparently real, more seductive and more desirable as they produce rather than reflect the reality in which we exist: contemporary subjectivity and society is not the producer of simulations, but the product of them. In the order of simulation, meaning 'implodes' and we move from reality to hyperreality.

'Hyperreality', as Chapter 4 suggested, is a key term for Baudrillard, and one that is crucial to grasp if his work is to be understood. It does not mean 'unreality', but rather identifies a culture in which the fantastical creations of media, film and computer technologies have come to be more real for us, and to interact more fundamentally with our experiences and desires, than the hitherto predominant realities of nature or spiritual life. In *Simulations*, Baudrillard argues that as a result of the contemporary advances in information technology, the real is now 'produced from miniaturised units, from matrices, memory banks and command models. . . . It is a hyperreal: the product of an irradiating synthesis of combinatory models in a hyperspace without atmosphere' (1983a: 3). He produces a helpful example of how third-order simulation operates to generate hyperreality in a discussion of the Californian theme park, Disneyland:

> Disneyland is there to conceal the fact that it is the 'real' country, all of the 'real' America, which *is* Disneyland. . . . Disneyland is present as imaginary in order to make us believe that the rest is real, when in fact all of Los Angeles and the America surrounding it are no longer real, but of the order of the hyperreal and simulation. It is no longer a question of a false representation of reality (ideology), but of concealing the fact that the real is no longer real . . .
>
> (1983a: 25)

For Baudrillard, Disneyland is not a fantasy that makes the mundane everyday reality of American life more bearable: it does not stand in opposition to or provide a place to escape from the 'real world'. Rather, it is a means of masking the fantastical nature of day-to-day existence in all of American society: it is, he claims, 'a deterrence machine set up in order to rejuvenate in reverse the fiction of the real' (1983a: 25). There is no longer any access to reality within American culture, but only the continual clash of simulations that form part of the infinitely seductive code of hyperreality. The function of Disneyland is to conceal this, to prevent the public from recognising the 'fact that the real is no longer real'.

This inversion of our expectations about the logic of representation is the essence of Baudrillard's notion of the 'implosion of meaning' in post-modern hyperreality. The same logic is employed in *Simulations* to argue, variously, that the function of prisons is to delude us into thinking that those on the outside are somehow free, and that political scandals such as the Watergate affair in 1970s America, in which the President was found to have been spying on his critics, serve mainly to delude the public that the entire body politic is not riddled with corruption. The point is that in the contemporary media-dominated world, everything partakes of fantasy, incarceration and corruption, and reality, freedom and truth have been banished entirely from day-to-day existence.

Baudrillard's arguments about simulation and hyperreality reached their most controversial conclusions in three essays he wrote before, during and just after the first Gulf War in 1991, which were collected together in his book *The Gulf War Did Not Take Place* (1995). Here Baudrillard argues that the incredible proliferation of spectacular images and seemingly instantaneous reports that formed the world media's saturation coverage of the war in Kuwait, instead of providing infor-mation about its reality, generated a vast masquerade of contradictory signs that transformed it into a virtual conflict: a war of hyperreal simulations from which the truth of suffering and death was rigorously excluded. These essays have become a *cause célèbre* argued over by proponents and opponents of postmodern theory.

For the anti-postmodernist critic Christopher Norris, these three texts, which form the central focus of his book *Uncritical Theory: Post-modernism, Intellectuals and the Gulf War*, are exemplary of what is wrong with postmodernism as a whole. He describes Baudrillard as a 'cult figure on the current "postmodernist" scene, and purveyor of some of the silliest ideas yet to gain a hearing' (Norris, 1992: 11), arguing that in the face of the clear evidence of violence, slaughter and destruction the claim that the war 'did not take place' is absurd and dangerously perverse.

Norris's is a powerfully written critique, but as a reading of Baudrillard's texts it has been accused by a number of critics of missing the point (see, for example, Patton, 1995: 15–20). Baudrillard does not deny the death or violence that took place, but rather raises the question of whether this can be called a 'war' in any sense that has accrued to the term in modern thought:

> Since this war was won in advance, we will never know what it would have been like had it existed. . . . We have seen what an ultra-modern process of electrocution is like, a process of paralysis and lobotomy of an experimental enemy away from the field of battle with no possibility of reaction. But this is not a war, any more than 10,000 tonnes of bombs per day is sufficient to make it a war. Any more than the direct transmission by CNN of real time information is sufficient to authenticate a war.
>
> (Baudrillard, 1995: 61)

Baudrillard's point in these essays is not to deny the violence, but rather to challenge the way in which the presentations of what happened sought to justify it according to the grand narrative categories of justice, freedom and the 'New World Order'. Instead, he reads it in terms of the logic of international media and capitalism as a promotional campaign for Western values and might: 'The media promotes the war, the war promotes the media, and advertising competes with the war . . . it allows us to turn the world and the violence of the world into a consumable substance' (1995: 31). The saturation coverage of the war across all media, the competition between the different media companies to acquire most quickly the most spectacular pictures and stories, and the ubiquity of advertising in all of the coverage, he argues, turn the war into a commodity. The infinite multiplication of representations, commentaries, arguments and images that this coverage gives rise to means, for Baudrillard, that the truth of and reasons for the conflict ceased to be important and, for the citizens of the West hypnotised by the simulations they were continually fed, a real understanding of what was taking place was impossible. In the face of this, Baudrillard argues, the task of the critic is to challenge the very discourses of truth and justice that gave rise to the events: 'If we do not have practical intelligence about the war (and none of us has), at least let us have a sceptical intelligence towards it, without renouncing the pathetic feeling of its absurdity' (1995: 58). In other words, the specific questions about what really did or did not happen are not just impossible to answer but also irrelevant; the key point, instead, from which critique must begin is a sceptical interrogation of the whole rhetoric of truth and falsity that surrounded its media representation.

It is less important here to decide whether Norris or Baudrillard is more correct about the specific events of the first Gulf War than to think through the philosophical principles that form the basis of their dis-agreement. For Norris, the problems emerge from postmodernism's denial of the foundational principles that are supplied by the ontological structure of the self-certain subject and the modern grand narratives. For Baudrillard, and this much at least he shares with most other postmodern thinkers, such foundational principles are precisely what needs to be challenged if a productive politics can emerge. The question for the postmodernist, then, must be: how is a politics that is not founded on the identity of the human subject and the progressive historical thinking of the grand narrative possible?

POSTMODERN POLITICS: RESISTANCE WITHOUT FOUNDATIONS

Jameson and Baudrillard in their relation to the Marxist heritage each propose a form of critique that attempts to work through the injustices of contemporary capitalism, by cognitive mapping and sceptical resistance to simulations respectively, without resorting to an oppositional grand narrative or positing the idea of an exterior and operative reality that lies behind some sort of contemporary false consciousness. For both thinkers, the search for the possibility of a postmodern political critique seems to call for modes of resistance that are immanent to capitalism itself rather than a politics that derives from a straightforwardly oppositional grand narrative that is based on alternative foundations.

For many thinkers who still adhere to modern Marxism, the notion of a politics that is not grounded in a foundational grand narrative is highly problematic. In a television interview broadcast in 1992, the British Marxist critic Terry Eagleton commented that it was ironic that 'at a time when . . . the system politically speaking has never been more total', postmodern theorists are refusing to think in terms of totality (Eagleton, 1992: 25). For Eagleton, the key problem with the postmodern analyses of fragmentation, simulation and hyperreality is that they fail to take account of the totality of social relations that give rise to contemporary

actuality. In other words, 'end-of-history thinking . . . its cultural relativism . . . its scepticism, pragmatism and localism, its distaste for ideas of
solidarity and disciplined organisation' fails to provide left politics with
the 'strong ethical and even anthropological foundations' (Eagleton,
1996: 134) it needs to confront the 'total systems' of today's politics. For
Eagleton, then, a radical politics must be both oppositional and foundational – the sort of alternative grand narrative that Marx's modern
philosophy developed. In contrast to this, a postmodern critique develops
a 'politics without foundations' that seeks other resources to resist
contemporary totalities.

Perhaps the clearest formulation of this sort of politics is given in an
essay, 'Politics and the Limits of Modernity', by the post-Marxist theorist
Ernesto Laclau. In this essay, he sets out to explore the ways in which a
postmodern criticism might challenge the modern without necessarily
giving up on its emancipatory aims. He argues that for contemporary
political theory,

> it is precisely the *ontological status* of the central categories of the
> discourse of modernity, and not their *content*, that is at stake; that the
> erosion of this status is expressed through the 'postmodern' sensibility;
> and that this erosion, far from being a negative phenomenon, repre-
> sents an enormous amplification of the content and operability of the
> values of modernity. . . . Postmodernity does not imply a *change* in
> the values of Enlightenment modernity but rather a particular weak-
> ening of their absolutist character.
>
> (Laclau, 1988: 66–7)

What he is getting at here is that the move from the modern to the
postmodern does not mark a loss of values such as justice, freedom or
truth, but rather a change in what he calls their 'ontological status': their
certainty, the means by which they are defined, justified and defended.
Lyotard makes a similar point in *The Postmodern Condition*, when he
argues that although universal consensus is no longer possible, 'justice as a
value is neither outmoded nor suspect. We must thus arrive at an idea and
practice of justice that is not linked to that of consensus' (1984: 66). For
both thinkers, the point is simple: one should not give up on values such
as freedom and justice, but one must approach them differently so that

they can be conceived and practised without the need to resort to the universal, absolutist categories of 'Man', totality or the grand narrative.

Laclau argues that what differentiates the postmodern from the modern is that, while the latter bases its projects on the 'notion of the totality of history', postmodernity 'begins when this fully present identity is threatened by an ungraspable exterior that introduces a dimension of opacity and pragmatism into the pretended immediacy and transparency of its categories' (1988: 72). The consequence of this is that the disruption of the foundational totalities of modern thought makes way for a 'plurality of contexts that redefine them in unpredictable ways' (1988: 72). A number of the arguments in the book have already explored what Laclau is evoking here: the postmodern sublime that presents the fact of the unpresentable's existence, the disruptions of Cartesian subjectivity in feminist and postcolonial discourse as well as the notions of performative pluralities and technological transformations of identity, and the fracturing of the grand narrative sweep of Hegelian history in the postmodern focus on history as a collection of finite narratives and historiographic metafictions. Each of these resists the impulse of modern thought to provide foundations or produce totalities, exploring instead the possibilities of plurality and fragmentation.

For Laclau, this acceptance of fracturing and disruption refocuses political analysis on 'the complex strategic-discursive operations implied by their affirmation and defence' (1988: 72). Using the evocative example of a society threatened with invasion by an outside power, he argues that a lack of certainty about where the enemy is going to attack does not lead to passivity and inaction but rather to a tactical analysis of the possibilities inherent in the available, and almost certainly incomplete, evidence. Likewise, a postmodern critic who refuses the certainty provided by a foundational grand narrative is not entirely at a loss about how to say anything useful about anything, but instead draws evidence from the whole range of social structures and signs: 'the transition from argument as discovery [of fundamental principles] to argument as a social construction entails a necessary modification of the *type of argument*' (Laclau, 1988: 79). Arguments, analyses and critiques thus become interventions in or, to borrow Jameson's and Baudrillard's terms, cognitive mappings of and sceptical resistances to the field of culture. The types of argument produced by a postmodern politics might be different, but they remain interventions in the world rather than, as they are sometimes accused of being by postmodernism's detractors, abdications from involvement.

The result of this transformation of types of argument, Laclau argues, is that critique moves from a foundational to a 'horizonal' structure. By 'horizon', he means the following:

> A formation that is unified in relation to a horizon is a formation without foundation: it constitutes itself as a unity only as it delimits itself from that which it negates. The discourses of equality and rights, for example, need not rely on a common human essence as their foundation; it suffices to posit an egalitarian logic whose limits of operation are given by the concrete argumentative practices existing in society. A horizon, then, is an empty locus, a point in which society symbolises its very groundlessness, in which concrete argumentative practices operate over a backdrop of radical freedom, of radical contingency.
>
> (Laclau, 1988: 81)

Postmodern critique produces the field in which it intervenes: it occurs without the stable ground of a grand narrative, but it emerges in the context of those narratives to challenge and subvert them. As Lyotard's discussion of the meaning of 'post-' in Chapter 2 argued, the postmodern exists in a problematic entanglement with a continuing modernity, the certainties and totalising gestures of which it attempts to disrupt from within. For both Laclau and Lyotard, then, the postmodern is not simply a move beyond the modern but is rather a mode of critique that is immanent to it. It does not provide final answers or set up alternative grand narratives. Instead, postmodernism in art, theory or culture generally sets out to demonstrate the fractures and silences that have always been part of the grand narratives, to present the violence that emerges from foundational thinking as its categories are imposed on the refractory world of experience, to find means to give voice to those subjects or aspects of subjectivity whose uniqueness is occluded or silenced by the discursive totalities of the modern.

Eagleton is right, 'the system politically speaking has never been more total' than it is today: multinational capitalism and the world markets are eroding the differences between cultures at an ever-accelerating rate, advances in technology may soon make the human obsolete, and the grand narratives are still evoked in order to impose their injunctions upon us. Most recently, the world has been given a choice: with no sense of irony, George W. Bush announced that, in the war on terrorism, 'You're either for us or against us' – accept everything that is done by us in your name or join the terrorists. For the postmodernist, this is a false choice, a totalising opposition that should be resisted. As Lyotard argues,

> The nineteenth and twentieth centuries have given us as much terror as we can take. We have paid a high enough price for the nostalgia of the whole and the one. . . . Under the general demand for slackening and for appeasement, we can hear the mutterings of the desire for a return of terror, for the realisation of the fantasy to seize reality. The answer is: let us wage a war on totality; let us be witnesses to the unpresentable; let us activate the differences and save the honour of the name.
>
> (1984: 81–2)

If there is a definition of postmodern politics, this is perhaps the closest we can get. The consequences of postmodern resistances are not fixed in advance, nor are the political allegiances of its critics: as the discussion of Fukuyama in Chapter 4 showed, there are right-wing as well as left-wing postmodernists. What the different forms of postmodern art, culture and theory do seem to share, however, is the desire to disturb, to challenge and to disrupt the totalising gestures that continually threaten to consume us.

GLOSSARY

Aesthetics The sphere of philosophy that explores, in its narrow sense, the experience of beauty and sublimity in art and nature, and, more generally, the whole structure of human sensation and perception that lies outside of the formation of clearly defined concepts (which are the stuff of epistemology).

Avant-garde An artistic movement that sets out to change the rules of art, test the limits of representation and style, and confront the public's expectations about what works of art should be. Often associated with modernism, the term is drawn from military language (the 'advanced guard' of an army) to identify those who lead in the battle to make things new.

Bourgeoisie Generally taken to refer to a middle-class person, but Marx's more specific definition identifies the bourgeoisie as those elements of society that own and control the means of production (the factories etc.) and their representatives in law and government.

Commodity An object used in exchange. For Karl Marx, a commodity denotes an object that is appreciated solely in terms of its exchange value: its inherent qualities are irrelevant, and it is seen solely in terms of its potential to be bought and sold. For some postmodern theorists, it is not just objects but also images, ideas and people that are in danger of being reduced entirely to commodities by international capitalism.

Cyborg A cyborg is a mixture of human and machine. Often the subject of science fiction, some postmodern thinkers argue that recent advances in science and technology are rapidly making the figure of the cyborg one that is becoming part of social reality.

Discourse A widely used and often vague term, but one that is vital to modern and postmodern theory. It is used in this book to identify particular critical systems and vocabularies that are employed to explain social formations, institutions and the practices that accompany them. So, for example, Marxism produces a discourse of modernity not just in its explanations of modern history and politics, but also in the ways that it proposes and generates specific forms of resistance to certain economic and political practices.

Enlightenment A movement that emerged during the seventeenth century which developed from the scientific and philosophical revolutions of the time and sought to use reason to liberate humanity from mysticism and superstition. It aimed to answer the key questions of human existence, meaning and morality through rational discourse and scientific explanation. Central to the Enlightenment tradition is the idea that history is a progress shaped by human beings towards a more informed and just future. It was the key precursor to philosophical modernity, and still holds sway in many areas of critical enquiry today.

Epistemology The branch of philosophy that enquires into knowledge and truth. It investigates what makes knowledge of the world possible, how such knowledge can be assumed to be shared between different people, and how truth can be differentiated from falsity.

Ethics The field of philosophical thought that examines the differences between good and evil, the principles of human duty and morality, and the logical bases of rights and justice.

Globalisation A somewhat controversial term that has been defined in a number of ways by theorists with different political perspectives. A relatively unproblematic definition might be Ulrich Beck's: 'denotes the *processes* through which sovereign national states are criss-crossed and undermined by transnational actors with varying prospects of power, orientations, identities and networks' (Beck, 2000: 101).

Hegemony Like ideology, hegemony designates the ways in which a social order functions by the consent as well as the coercion of its citizens. This consent is generated by civil institutions such as schools, the church and the media that instil shared sets of beliefs and values in the populace. For some Marxists, a key part of the revolutionary struggle is the transformation of bourgeois hegemony through the education of the proletariat.

Humanism An understanding of the world based on the recognition that human beings are the basis of knowledge and action, and have inherent value, dignity and free will. It emerged as a cultural movement in fourteenth-century Europe, and came to be strongly associated with the Enlightenment's attempts to emancipate 'Man' from spiritual or religious mysticism. For a number of modern and postmodern thinkers, humanist philosophy has been an important target for criticism.

Ideology In general terms, an ideology is a set of beliefs and attitudes held (whether consciously or not) by an individual or community which shapes their understanding and ethical response to others. In its more specifically Marxist usage, ideology denotes a false consciousness of one's relation to the forces and relations of production, and thus of one's place in society.

Logocentrism A term coined by the French philosopher Jacques Derrida to denote the philosophies that are based on the idea that meaning is immediate and stable, and that words and signs communicate directly and naturally. This idea has come under attack from both modern and postmodern theorists who conceive meaning as socially, culturally and historically mutable.

Metaphysics The branch of philosophy that deals with first principles and essences. It is often presented as the ultimate science of existence, reality and knowledge because it enquires into the conditions of their possibility.

Ontology A branch of philosophical enquiry that investigates the meaning of being and existence. A key example of ontological investigation is that undertaken by René Descartes in *Meditations*.

Parody A parody is a work that through mimicry (either subtle or grotesque) of another's style demonstrates the latter's absurdity. For Jameson, parody is a modernist style, whereas for Hutcheon it is part of postmodernism.

Pastiche Like parody, pastiche borrows ideas or stylistic devices from another work or works. Unlike parody, pastiche does not imply any mockery or criticism of the works that it incorporates. According to Jameson, pastiche is a vital aspect of postmodernism.

Proletariat Generally understood as the working class. Marx defines them more precisely as wage earners: those without access to capital or control of the means of production who have to sell their labour. For Marxism, the proletariat is the 'revolutionary class'.

Relativism The argument that truth and morality are relative rather than firmly fixed, that particular truths and ethical principles are posited on the basis of sets of beliefs (or even ideologies) held by a culture rather than necessary or actual. In other words, truth is based on conventions and beliefs rather than absolute principles.

Subject/subjectivity In its most simple terms, a subject is a human being; however the term itself has important resonances. The Latin term 'subjectum', from which 'subject' derives, means 'that which lies under', and indicates that which persists through change. In grammar, the subject is the part of the sentence that performs the actions on the object. Combining both of these meanings, 'subject' in modern thought is usually taken to indicate an active human agent who is capable of reflecting rationally upon her or his actions and existence. In postmodern theory a third meaning of 'subject' is presented alongside the first two: to be subjected is to be made to submit to an external force or agency. In the relation between the modern and the postmodern, the question of what a subject is forms a key point of contention. (See Chapter 3 for a detailed discussion.)

Sublime Along with the beautiful, the sublime is a category of aesthetics. An experience is sublime if it generates a mixture of exhilaration and terror through the sense that it might overwhelm or obliterate the subject. Because of its potential to disrupt expectations and the everyday flow of experience, it forms a vital aspect of many accounts of postmodernism.

Teleology The philosophical study of the ends and goals of nature and human action. Teleology investigates whether logical purposes can be found to underlie actions and events, and for some thinkers is explored as a means of proving that there is an ultimate purpose behind the world (God, fate, the rational, etc.).

Suggestions for Further Reading

The bibliography gives details of the full range of texts discussed during the book, all of which will be relevant to anyone interested in the postmodern. Some of these are more accessible than others, however. The following is a list of texts that might provide useful and accessible starting points for further reading about some of the key aspects of postmodern theory.

Berman, Marshall (1982) *All that is Solid Melts into Air: The Experience of Modernity*, London: Verso. [An accessible and often fascinating introduction to the literature and politics of nineteenth- and twentieth-century modernity that sets the scene for many contemporary debates about the modern and the postmodern.]

Bertens, Hans (1995) *The Idea of the Postmodern: A History*, London: Routledge. [A detailed and wide-ranging introduction to postmodern culture, theory and sociology.]

Connor, Steven (1997) *Postmodernist Culture: An Introduction to Theories of the Contemporary*, 2nd edition, Oxford: Blackwell. [A very detailed introduction to the culture of postmodernism which provides in-depth discussions of topics ranging from legal theory to popular television, and produces a coherent account of the contemporary arts.]

Harvey, David (1990) *The Condition of Postmodernity*, Oxford: Blackwell. [An influential and always accessible sociological analysis of the economic and political implications of postmodern theory and culture.]

Heartney, Eleanor (2001) *Postmodernism*, London: Tate Gallery Publishing. [A clear and widely ranging introduction to the theories of postmodern art which is helpfully accompanied by reproductions of many of the works discussed.]

Lyon, David (1999) *Postmodernity*, 2nd edition, Buckingham: Open University Press. [A very accessible and interesting introduction to the politics and sociology of postmodernity.]

Norris, Christopher (1990) *What's Wrong with Postmodernism: Critical Theory and the Ends of Philosophy*, Hemel Hempstead: Harvester Wheatsheaf. [A detailed and often trenchant attack on postmodern philosophy that sets out to demonstrate that contemporary critical theory has lost touch with political critique. This is probably the clearest of the anti-postmodernism texts currently available.]

Sim, Stuart, ed. (2001) *The Routledge Companion to Postmodernism*, London: Routledge. [A very useful reference work on the postmodern that includes both a collection of essays on general themes and a series of shorter entries that introduce some of the key artists, theorists and ideas associated with postmodernism.]

Sim, Stuart (2002) *Irony and Crisis: A Critical History of Postmodern Culture*, Cambridge: Icon. [Described as a 'sourcebook', this accessible introduction to postmodern theory and culture quotes extensively from some of the key theoretical texts associated with contemporary theory and offers brief but helpful commentaries on them.]

Woods, Tim (1999) *Beginning Postmodernism*, Manchester: Manchester University Press. [A very straightforward introduction to postmodern theory and culture aimed at undergraduate students, which includes helpful 'Stop and Think' sections that revise some of the key ideas.]

Also extremely useful are the introductions to individual theorists included in the *Routledge Critical Thinkers* series. Each of these offers a straightforward introduction to the theorist's work and an exploration of their impact on modern thought and culture. Particularly relevant for readers interested in the postmodern are:

Lane, Richard J. (2000) *Jean Baudrillard*, London: Routledge.
Malpas, Simon (2003) *Jean-François Lyotard*, London: Routledge.
Roberts, Adam (2000) *Fredric Jameson*, London: Routledge.

BIBLIOGRAPHY

Aristotle (1965) *On the Art of Poetry*, in T.S. Dorsch, ed. and trans. (1965) *Aristotle, Horace, Longinus: Classical Literary Criticism*, Harmondsworth: Penguin, pp. 29–75.

Atkins, Barry (2003) *More than a Game: The Computer Game as Fictional Form*, Manchester: Manchester University Press.

Barnes, Peter (1989) *Plays: One*, London: Methuen.

—— (1989) *Red Noses*, London: Faber and Faber.

Baudrillard, Jean (1975) *The Mirror of Production*, trans. Mark Poster, St Louis: Telos.

—— (1983a) *Simulations*, trans. Paul Foss, Paul Patton and Philip Beitchman, New York: Semiotext(e).

—— (1983b) *In the Shadow of the Silent Majorities: Or, the End of the Social and Other Essays*, trans. Paul Foss, Paul Patton and John Johnston, New York: Semiotext(e).

—— (1990) *Seduction*, trans. B. Singer, London: Macmillan.

—— (1994) *The Illusion of the End*, trans. Chris Turner, Cambridge: Polity Press.

—— (1995) *The Gulf War Did Not Take Place*, trans. Paul Patton, Sydney: Power.

—— (1998) *The Consumer Society: Myths and Structures*, London: Sage.

Bauman, Zygmunt (1993) *Postmodern Ethics*, Oxford: Blackwell.

—— (1995) *Life in Fragments: Essays in Postmodern Morality*, Oxford: Blackwell.

Beck, Ulrich (2000) 'What is Globalisation?' in David Held and Anthony McGrew, eds (2000) *The Global Transformations Reader: an Introduction to the Globalisation Debate*, Cambridge: Polity, pp. 99–103.

Belsey, Catherine (1980) *Critical Practice*, London: Routledge.

Belsey, Catherine and Jane Moore, eds (1989) *The Feminist Reader: Essays in Gender and the Politics of Literary Criticism*, London: Macmillan.

Benjamin, Walter (1973) *Illuminations*, trans. Harry Zohn, London: Fontana.

Berman, Marshall (1982) *All that is Solid Melts into Air: The Experience of Modernity*, London: Verso.

Bertens, Hans (1995) *The Idea of the Postmodern: A History*, London: Routledge.

Best, Steven and Douglas Kellner (2001) *The Postmodern Adventure: Science, Technology and Cultural Studies at the Third Millennium*, London: Routledge.

Bhabha, Homi (1986) 'Foreword: Remembering Fanon', in Frantz Fanon (1986) *Black Skin, White Masks*, trans. Charles Lam Markmann, London: Pluto Press, pp. vii–xxvi.

—— (1994) *The Location of Culture*, London: Routledge.

Bowie, Andrew (2003) *Aesthetics and Subjectivity from Kant to Nietzsche*, 2nd edition, Manchester: Manchester University Press.

Breton, André (1992) 'First Manifesto of Surrealism', in Charles Harrison and Paul Wood, eds (1992) *Art in Theory 1900 – 1990: An Anthology of Changing Ideas*, Oxford: Blackwell, pp. 432–9.

Brewster, Scott, John J. Joughin, David Owens and Richard J. Walker, eds (2000) *Inhuman Reflections: Thinking the Limits of the Human*, Manchester: Manchester University Press.

Burbach, Roger (2001) *Globalisation and Postmodern Politics: From Zapatistas to High-Tech Robber Barons*, London: Pluto.

Butler, Judith (1990) *Gender Trouble: Feminism and the Subversion of Identity*, London: Routledge.

Butler, Rex (1999) *Jean Baudrillard: The Defence of the Real*, London: Sage.

Callinicos, Alex (1989) *Against Postmodernism: A Marxist Critique*, Cambridge: Polity Press.

Carroll, Lewis (2003) *Alice's Adventures in Wonderland, and Through the Looking-Glass*, Harmondsworth: Penguin.

Carter, Angela (1984) *Nights at the Circus*, London: Chatto & Windus.

Cervantes (1950) *Don Quixote*, trans. J.M. Cohen, Harmondsworth: Penguin.

Cixous, Hélène (1986) 'Sorties: Out and Out: Attacks/Ways Out/Forays', in Hélène Cixous and Catherine Clément (1986) *The Newly Born Woman*, trans. Betsy Wing, Minneapolis: University of Minnesota Press, pp. 63–132.

Hélène Cixous and Catherine Clément (1986) *The Newly Born Woman*, trans. Betsy Wing, Minneapolis: University of Minnesota Press.

Coetzee, J.M. (1987) *Foe*, Harmondsworth: Penguin.

Connor, Steven (1997) *Postmodernist Culture: An Introduction to Theories of the Contemporary*, 2nd edition, Oxford: Blackwell.

Conrads, Ulrich, ed. (1970) *Programs and Manifestoes on Twentieth-Century Architecture*, Cambridge, Mass.: MIT Press.

Danto, Arthur C. (1992) *Beyond the Brillo Box: The Visual Arts in Post-Historical Perspective*, Berkeley, Calif. and London: University of California Press.

Debord, Guy (2002) *The Society of the Spectacle*, trans. Donald Nicholson-Smith, New York: Zone Books.

Derrida, Jacques (1994) *Specters of Marx: The State of Debt, the Work of Mourning, and the New International*, trans. Peggy Kamuf, London: Routledge.

Descartes, René (1968) *Discourse on Method and the Meditations*, ed. and trans. F.E. Sutcliffe, Harmondsworth: Penguin.

Dorsch, T.S., ed. and trans. (1965) *Aristotle, Horace, Longinus: Classical Literary Criticism*, Harmondsworth: Penguin.

Eagleton, Terry (1990) *The Ideology of the Aesthetic*, Oxford: Blackwell.

—— (1992) Interview in Rod Stoneman and Jonathan Rée, eds, *Talking Liberties*, London: Channel 4 Publications.

—— (1996) *The Illusions of Postmodernism*, Oxford: Blackwell.

Easthope, Antony (1999) *The Unconscious*, London: Routledge.

Elam, Diane (1992) *Romancing the Postmodern*, London: Routledge.

Fanon, Frantz (1986) *Black Skin, White Masks*, trans. Charles Lam Markmann, London: Pluto Press.

Foster, Hal, ed. (1985) *Postmodern Culture*, London: Pluto Press.

Frampton, Kenneth (1985) 'Towards a Critical Regionalism: Six Points for an

Architecture of Resistance', in Hal Foster, ed. (1985) *Postmodern Culture*, London: Pluto Press, pp. 16–30.

Freud, Sigmund (1984) *On Metapsychology: The Theory of Psychoanalysis*, ed. Angela Richards, trans. James Strachey, Harmondsworth: Penguin.

Fukuyama, Francis (1991) 'Changed Days for Ruritania's Dictator', *The Guardian*, 8 April, p. 19.

—— (1992) *The End of History and the Last Man*, Harmondsworth: Penguin.

Gibson, William (1995) *Neuromancer*, London: HarperCollins.

Grass, Günter (1989a) *The Tin Drum*, trans. Ralph Manheim, London: Picador.

—— (1989b) *Cat and Mouse*, trans. Ralph Manheim, London: Picador.

—— (1989c) *Dog Years*, trans. Ralph Manheim, London: Picador.

Gray, Alasdair (1992) *Poor Things*, Harmondsworth: Penguin.

Gray, Henry (1980) *Gray's Anatomy*, Edinburgh: Churchill Livingstone.

Greenberg, Clement (1986–96) *Clement Greenberg: The Collected Essays and Criticism*, 4 vols, ed. John O'Brian, Chicago and London: University of Chicago Press.

Habermas, Jürgen (1987) *The Philosophical Discourse of Modernity: Twelve Lectures*, trans. Frederick Lawrence, Cambridge: Polity Press.

—— (1996) 'Modernity: An Unfinished Project', in Maurizio Passerin d'Entrèves and Seyla Benhabib (1996) *Habermas and the Unfinished Project of Modernity: Critical Essays on The Philosophical Discourse of Modernity*, Cambridge: Polity Press, pp. 38–55.

Hamilton, Paul (1996) *Historicism*, London: Routledge.

Haraway, Donna J. (1991) *Simians, Cyborgs, and Women: The Reinvention of Nature*, London: Free Association Books.

Harrison, Charles and Wood, Paul (1992) *Art in Theory 1900–1990: An Anthology of Changing Ideas*, Oxford: Blackwell.

Harvey, David (1990) *The Condition of Postmodernity*, Oxford: Blackwell.

Hassan, Ihab (1982) *The Dismemberment of Orpheus: Toward a Postmodern Literature*, 2nd edition, New York: Oxford University Press.

—— (1987) *The Postmodern Turn: Essays in Postmodern Theory and Culture*, Columbus: Ohio State University Press.

Heartney, Eleanor (2001) *Postmodernism*, London: Tate Gallery Publishing.

Hegel, G.W.F. (1952) *Philosophy of Right*, trans. T.M. Knox, Oxford: Clarendon Press.

—— (1975) *Lectures on the Philosophy of World History. Introduction: Reason in History*, trans. H.B. Nisbett, Cambridge: Cambridge University Press.

—— (1977) *Phenomenology of Spirit*, trans. A.V. Miller, Oxford: Oxford University Press.

Heidegger, Martin (1977) *The Question Concerning Technology and Other Essays*, trans. William Lovitt, London: Harper & Row.

Held, David and Anthony McGrew, eds (2000) *The Global Transformations Reader: An Introduction to the Globalisation Debate*, Cambridge: Polity.

Herodotus (1972) *The Histories*, trans. E. de Selincourt, Harmondsworth: Penguin.

Hutcheon, Linda (1988) *The Poetics of Postmodernism: History, Theory, Fiction*, London: Routledge.

—— (2002) *The Politics of Postmodernism*, 2nd edition, London: Routledge.

Huyssen, Andreas (1986) *After the Great Divide: Modernism, Mass Culture, Postmodernism*, London: Macmillan.

Jameson, Fredric (1983) 'Postmodernism and Consumer Society' in Hal Foster, ed. (1985) *Postmodern Culture*, London: Pluto Press, pp. 111–25.

—— (1990) *Late Marxism: Adorno, or the Persistence of the Dialectic*, London: Verso.

—— (1991) *Postmodernism, or, the Cultural Logic of Late Capitalism*, London: Verso.

—— (1992) *The Geopolitical Aesthetic: Cinema and Space in the World System*, Bloomington: Indiana University Press.

—— (2002) *A Singular Modernity: Essay on the Ontology of the Present*, London: Verso.

Jencks, Charles (1987) *Post-Modernism: The New Classicism in Art and Architecture*, London: Academy Editions.

—— (1991) *The Language of Post-Modern Architecture*, 6th edition, London: Academy Editions.

—— (1996) *What is Post-Modernism?*, 4th edition, London: Academy Editions.

Jenkins, Keith (2001) *Why History? Ethics and Postmodernity*, London: Routledge.

Joyce, James (1964) *Finnegans Wake*, 3rd edition, London: Faber.

—— (1969) *Ulysses*, Harmondsworth: Penguin.

Kant, Immanuel (1929) *Critique of Pure Reason*, trans. Norman Kemp Smith, London: Macmillan.

—— (1963) *On History*, ed. Lewis White Beck, London: Macmillan.

—— (1987) *Critique of Judgement*, trans. Werner S. Pluhar, Indianapolis and Cambridge: Hackett.

—— (1993) *Critique of Practical Reason*, trans. Lewis White Beck, New York and Basingstoke: Macmillan.

Kiefer, Anselm (2001) *The Seven Heavenly Palaces 1973–2001*, Basel: Hatje Cantz.

Klein, Naomi (2000) *No Logo*, London: Flamingo.

Kristeva, Julia (1989) 'Women's Time', in Catherine Belsey and Jane Moore, eds (1989) *The Feminist Reader: Essays in Gender and the Politics of Literary Criticism*, London: Macmillan, pp. 197–217.

Lacan, Jacques (1977a) *Écrits: A Selection*, trans. Alan Sheridan, London: Routledge.

—— (1977b) *The Four Fundamental Concepts of Psycho-Analysis*, trans. Alan Sheridan, Harmondsworth: Penguin.

—— (1982) *Feminine Sexuality: Jacques Lacan and the 'École Freudienne'*, trans. Jacqueline Rose, London: Macmillan.

Laclau, Ernesto (1988) 'Politics and the Limits of Modernity', in Andrew Ross, ed. (1988) *Universal Abandon? The Politics of Postmodernism*, Edinburgh: Edinburgh University Press, pp. 63–82.

Lane, Richard J. (2000) *Jean Baudrillard*, London: Routledge.

Lash, Scott (1990) *Sociology of Postmodernism*, London: Routledge.

Lukács, Georg (1969) *The Historical Novel*, trans. Hannah and Stanley Mitchell, Harmondsworth: Penguin.

Lyon, David (1999) *Postmodernity*, 2nd edition, Buckingham: Open University Press.

Lyotard, Jean-François (1984) *The Postmodern Condition: A Report on Knowledge*, trans. Geoffrey Bennington and Brian Massumi, Manchester: Manchester University Press.

—— (1988) *The Differend: Phrases in Dispute*, trans. Georges Van Den Abeele, Manchester: Manchester University Press.

—— (1991) *The Inhuman: Reflections on Time*, trans. Geoffrey Bennington and Rachel Bowlby, Cambridge: Polity Press.

—— (1992) *The Postmodern Explained*, trans. Don Barry, Bernadette Maher, Julian Pefanis, Virginia Spate and Morgan Thomas, Minneapolis: University of Minnesota Press.

—— (1993) *Libidinal Economy*, trans. Iain Hamilton Grant, London: Athlone.

—— (1997) *Postmodern Fables*, trans. Georges Van Den Abeele, Minneapolis: University of Minnesota Press.

—— (2000) *The Confession of Augustine*, trans. Richard Beardsworth, Stanford, Calif.: Stanford University Press.

McHale, Brian (1987) *Postmodernist Fiction*, London: Methuen.

Malpas, Simon (2001) *Postmodern Debates*, Basingstoke: Palgrave.

—— (2003) *Jean-François Lyotard*, London: Routledge.

Mandel, Ernest (1978) *Late Capitalism*, London: New Left Books.

Marx, Karl (2000) *Selected Writings*, 2nd edition, ed. David McLellan, Oxford: Oxford University Press.

Marx, Karl and Friedrich Engels (1967) *The Communist Manifesto*, Harmondsworth: Penguin.

Monbiot, George (2000) *Captive State: The Corporate Takeover of Britain*, Basingstoke: Macmillan.

—— (2003) *The Age of Consent: A Manifesto for a New World Order*, London: Flamingo.

Nancy, Jean-Luc (1993) *The Birth to Presence*, trans. Brian Holmes *et al.*, Stanford, Calif.: Stanford University Press.

—— (1997) *The Sense of the World*, trans. Jeffrey S. Librett, Minneapolis: University of Minnesota Press.

Norris, Christopher (1990) *What's Wrong with Postmodernism: Critical Theory and the Ends of Philosophy*, Hemel Hempstead: Harvester Wheatsheaf.

—— (1992) *Uncritical Theory: Postmodernism, Intellectuals and the Gulf War*, London: Lawrence and Wishart.

—— (1993) *The Truth about Postmodernism*, Oxford: Blackwell.

Passerin d'Entrèves, Maurizio and Seyla Benhabib (1996) *Habermas and the Unfinished Project of Modernity: Critical Essays on The Philosophical Discourse of Modernity*, Cambridge: Polity Press.

Patton, Paul (1995) 'Introduction', in Jean Baudrillard (1995) *The Gulf War Did Not Take Place*, trans. Paul Patton, Sydney: Power, pp. 1–21.

Readings, Bill and Schaber, Bennet, eds (1993) *Postmodernism Across the Ages: Essays for a Postmodernity that Wasn't Born Yesterday*, Syracuse, NY: Syracuse University Press.

Roberts, Adam (2000) *Fredric Jameson*, London: Routledge.

Rosenblatt, Roger (2001) 'The Age of Irony Comes to an End', *Time Magazine*, 158, 13 (24 September), p. 79.

Ross, Andrew, ed. (1988) *Universal Abandon? The Politics of Postmodernism*, Edinburgh: Edinburgh University Press.

Rushdie, Salman (1981) *Midnight's Children*, London: Cape.

—— (1983) *Shame*, London: Cape.

Russell, Bertrand (2000) *A History of Western Philosophy*, London: Routledge.

Said, Edward (1975) *Beginnings: Intention and Method*, New York: Basic Books.

—— (1985) *Orientalism*, Harmondsworth: Penguin.

Scott, Sir Walter (1985) *Waverley*, Harmondsworth: Penguin.

Sidney, Sir Philip (2002) *An Apology for Poetry, or The Defence of Poesy*, 3rd edition, ed. R.W. Maslen, Manchester: Manchester University Press.

Sim, Stuart, ed. (2001) *The Routledge Companion to Postmodernism*, London: Routledge.

—— (2002) *Irony and Crisis: A Critical History of Postmodern Culture*, Cambridge: Icon.

Smith, Adam (1986) *The Wealth of Nations: Books I–III*, Harmondsworth: Penguin.

Soper, Kate (1986) *Humanism and Anti-Humanism*, London: Hutchinson.

Sterne, Laurence (1983) *The Life and Opinions of Tristram Shandy*, Oxford: Oxford University Press.

Stiglitz, Joseph (2002) *Globalisation and its Discontents*, Harmondsworth: Penguin.

Thacker, Andrew (2003) *Moving through Modernity: Space, Geography and Modernism*, Manchester: Manchester University Press.

Toynbee, Arnold (1954) *A Study of History*, Vol. IX, Oxford: Oxford University Press.

Vattimo, Gianni (1988) *The End of Modernity: Nihilism and Hermeneutics in Post-Modern Culture*, trans. Jon R. Snyder, Cambridge: Polity Press.

White, Hayden (1978) *Tropics of Discourse: Essays in Cultural Criticism*, Baltimore: Johns Hopkins University Press.

—— (1986) 'Historical Pluralism', *Critical Inquiry*, 12, 3, pp. 480–93.

Winterson, Jeanette (1992) *Written on the Body*, London: Jonathan Cape.

Woods, Tim (1999) *Beginning Postmodernism*, Manchester: Manchester University Press.

Wordsworth, William (1995) *The Prelude: The Four Texts (1798, 1799, 1805, 1850)*, ed. Jonathan Wordsworth, Harmondsworth: Penguin.

INDEX